W. Cramer

The Christian Father

What He Should Be, And What He Should Do

W. Cramer

The Christian Father
What He Should Be, And What He Should Do

ISBN/EAN: 9783744659604

Printed in Europe, USA, Canada, Australia, Japan

Cover: Foto ©Lupo / pixelio.de

More available books at **www.hansebooks.com**

What he should be, and what he should do.

TOGETHER WITH A COLLECTION OF

Prayers Suitable to his Condition.

TRANSLATED FROM THE GERMAN OF
RIGHT REV. W CRAMER, D.D.,
Coadjutor Bishop of Münster.

BY

REV. L. A. LAMBERT,
Pastor of St. Mary's Church, Waterloo, N. Y.

WITH AN INTRODUCTION BY

RIGHT REV. STEPHEN V. RYAN, D.D., C.M.,
Bishop of Buffalo.

TWENTY-FIFTH THOUSAND

New York, Cincinnati, and Chicago:
BENZIGER BROTHERS,
Printers to the Holy Apostolic See.

Imprimatur.

JOHN, CARDINAL McCLOSKEY,

Archbishop of New York.

COPYRIGHT, 1883, BY BENZIGER BROTHERS.

INTRODUCTION.

The appearance of "The Christian Father" in an English dress we hail with sincerest pleasure, and we doubt not that it will meet a warm welcome from the English-speaking community. Its companion volume, "The Christian Mother," has met with well-deserved favor, and has found its way into many a Christian home, to cheer and to bless it. "The Christian Father" must be equally popular and equally beneficial, for it is equally admirable for its practical good sense, winning simplicity, and deeply religious lessons. It is no mere ideal father we have here, aspiring after unattainable or fanciful saintliness. It is a father such as God intended all fathers to be, such as should and might be found at the head of every Christian family. It is a genuine Christian father faithfully discharging the obligations of his state and sanctifying himself in the ordinary every-day duties of life. If in the family and in society God's holy providence has allotted to the mother a place which only the Christian mother can fill, with much more reason may we say the same of the father. A father, becoming under God the principle of existence to others, shares with the great Creator and Father of all the noblest prerogative of which a creature is capable, that of paternity or fatherhood. The father actually holds the place of God, and exercises an authority subordinate only to that of God, over his children, and in return he rightfully challenges and instinctively receives respect and honor approximating the honor paid to God himself. With inborn reverence and confiding trust the child looks up to the father as the sum of all power, knowledge, and perfection. Great indeed, then, must be the responsibilities, most sacred the duties, which God and nature impose on the father. He must try hard to realize the child's ideal and put on the character of Him whom he represents. It is a mysterious but undeniable fact that children are left entirely in the hands and, we may say, at the mercy of the parents who beget them, for life, physical constitution, native character, and moral training. To the father, as head of the family, and invested with God-like powers and divine rights, it is given to exercise a controlling influence; he shapes the destinies, he moulds the characters of his offspring. As a general rule, children are what their father makes them. Like begets like. But the father not only transmits to his offspring a great resemblance to himself in form and feature, temperament, constitution, and natural disposition, he moreover unconsciously communicates to his children his own habits of thought, his likes and dislikes, his religious sentiments and moral principles, whilst his children in after-years recall his examples, his actions, and his words, by which to rule and square their own conduct and lives. The Christian father will naturally instil Christian habits, impart a moral tone, and infuse a religious spirit into his family; and as the family is the foundation of society, we must make the father truly Christian would we reform society, Christianize the land, or make the people moral. How can Christianity flourish; how can public or private virtue prevail; how can morality exist among the people, if fathers who have the moulding of the future generations, the training and education of children, under their almost exclusive control, are unprincipled or immoral men, unchristian, irreligious, or sensual? Give us, on the contrary, Christian fathers, and we shall soon have well-reared families, happy and virtuous homes. None are more alive to the pressing need of good Christian fathers than the ministers of religion, whose calling brings them so often into contact with wretchedness and sin. This, doubtless, it was that impelled the Rev. W. Cramer, a holy and learned man, who for years has been the educator, counsellor, and guide of the Clergy of the Diocese of Münster, to publish the excellent little work "The Christian Father" now for the first time given to the English-speaking public. He draws a life-like portrait of the true Christian father, shows the sublimity of his calling, explains his duties and obligations, the difficulties and dangers to which he is exposed, the graces which he needs for the sanctification of himself and his household, and the means which he must employ in order to secure those needed graces. May God bless the good Priest for this little gem of a book! May it find its way into every Christian home in the land, and may every Catholic father in America exemplify in his life "The Christian Father"!

✢ S. V. RYAN,
Bishop of Buffalo.
Feast of the Circumcision, 1883.

CONTENTS.

	PAGE
Introduction	3
The Name of Father	11
The Father's Vocation	23
His Stewardship	23
His Qualifications	33
The August Nature of his Vocation	35
The Christian Father	42
The Christian Mother Alone not Sufficient	43
The Father must be Truly Christian	49
The Importance of this Obligation	57
The Model Christian Father.—Sketch	60
A Word to the Heart of the Father	64
The Full Picture	73
How may it be Realized?	79
But let Us be Just	85

Contents.

	PAGE
Completion of the Picture	88
The Difficulties not to be Increased without Necessity	88
Avoid Danger	92
I. Dangers to Faith	92
II. Visiting Public-houses	96
Fail not to Practise the Christian Life	104
1. In what does it Consist?	105
2. Prayer	108
3. Keep Holy the Sabbath Day	113
4. "Arise and Eat"	117
The Work of the Christian Father	122
I. Gather to Yourself Treasures	125
II. Government.—Discipline	134
1. Law, Rule, and Order	136
2. See that Rules are Observed	145
3. Punishment	149
III. Paternal Cares	163
1. Superintendence of Children	163
2. The Son and Daughter Abroad	171
3. Choice of a State of Life	180
Two Model Fathers	194

Contents.

	PAGE
I. Abraham.—Mixed Marriages	194
II. Tobias	204
The Farmer of Münster	210
The Father at Prayer	228

PART II.

PRAYERS.

Prayer for Piety and Fear of God	237
Prayer for the Grace of Faith	238
Prayer to Obtain the Virtue of Temperance	240
Prayer against Inordinate Love of the World	241
Prayer for Marriage Anniversary	243
Morning Prayer	246
Evening Prayer	247
Prayers at Mass	249
Prayer for Wisdom	253
Prayer for Mildness	255
Prayer to Jesus, the Friend of Children	256
Prayer to the Blessed Virgin	257
Prayer to St. Joseph	258
Prayer to the Guardian Angel	258

	PAGE
Prayer to the Patron Saint of Children.....	259
A Father's Prayer for Blessings on His Work..................	260
Prayer for Protection of Children in Temptation...............................	261
A Prayer to Preserve Children from Mortal Sin..................................	262
A Prayer for Purity in Children...........	263
Prayer of a Father for His Wife....	264
Litany of the Christian Father............	266
Prayer to the Sacred Heart of Jesus.......	271
Prayer to the Sacred Heart of Mary.......	273
Prayer to St. Aloysius....	275

THE CHRISTIAN FATHER.

The Name of Father.

"Father:"—one of the first words uttered by infant lips, the first fruit, as it were, of the precious gift of speech, offered in honor of the Father in heaven and the father on earth, to whom we are indebted for existence and language.

Father: what a venerable name! It was pronounced from all eternity to express the mysterious relationship existing between the first two persons of the Deity. When God called men into being they addressed him by the name of "Father." And such he was; for he made them his children, and as his children he endowed them with the highest gifts.

And when by sin they lost this high privilege of being children of God, he himself, in the second person of the Trinity, came down upon earth and restored to them that holy prerogative. This was the precious fruit of the life and works, the suffering and death of the Redeemer. "As many as believed in him, to them he gave power to become children of God." God was, and is again in the fullest sense of the word, "Father" of all those who in the holy church are reborn children of God. Our divine Redeemer taught us to know him again as Father. He called him "Our heavenly Father"—"Our Father who art in heaven." In like manner should his faithful disciples, following his example, address him when they pray, as "Our Father who art in heaven." God, the Father of men! As many as are born again of water and the Holy Ghost are his children, and he is their Father.

How justly is this title his! Is it not to him that all men owe existence and life? And if by baptism they have acquired a supernatural sonship to God, is it not he who in the person of the Holy Ghost created them anew? It is he who must support and lead to a higher perfection that natural and supernatural life which was given by him, if it is to exist and arrive at perfection at all. He is in truth the Father of men, and we are his children.

But he has not willed to appropriate to himself exclusively this fatherhood, or the august title of Father. As he stamped upon all men the image of his divine nature and made them in his own likeness, so, according to the decree of his divine wisdom and love, his fatherhood should have its image in humanity; a certain number among men should participate in the privileges and prerogatives of his paternal dignity; they also should be fathers and have children. As to him so also to them should children owe their being. As he created his children in his natural and supernatural likeness, so also should fathers communicate to their children a part of their material as well as spiritual nature. As he by never failing grace seeks to lead his children to ever higher degrees of perfection, so also should fathers, by salutary influence, take part in this work of sanctification and perfection. As he from all eternity has the happy consciousness that all those who are by him and with him eternally happy owe their happiness and salvation to him, so should the human father also, when in heaven, have the consciousness that by fulfilling his paternal duties he has assisted his children to gain the happiness of heaven.

Every human father, then, is an image of the great Father in heaven, his divinely appointed representative on earth. "All paternity in heaven and on earth is from God," says the Apostle. And what he says of worldly authority is in a higher sense true in reference to a father and to the paternal dignity. "There is no power but from God, and those who are, are ordained of God." Now the father is an image and representative of the great Father who is in heaven; he therefore partakes of the prerogative of the divine fatherhood; he stands above his children; he is their lord and ruler; he has the title and right to honor, obedience, and subjection on the part of his children. They owe him reverence, obedience, and love as they owe them to God their heavenly Father, and are bound in consequence to render them. These words of the Lord have a particular value for fathers in relation to their children: "He that hears you, hears me; he that despises you, despises me." Could the great heavenly Father have honored more highly the human father, his representative on earth, than when he gave the commandment which refers to him the next place to those which refer to his own divine person? He also honored fathers (and mothers) in the fact that the commandment which refers to them is the only one which he accompanies with a positive promise: "Honor thy father (and thy mother) that it may be well with thee." What is more sublime than the expressions of the Holy Scriptures in which the Lord in manifold ways promises his heavenly blessings to children who obey their father (and mother)? On the other hand, what is more terrible than the curse which he utters against children who disobey, and are wanting in reverence to their father (and mother)? And have not these utterances been verified in sacred history? The choicest blessings for good children, and the most terrible afflictions for wicked sons and daughters. What the Scripture relates is proved by every-day experience.

And what follows from all this? Does it not follow that since God has imposed on children so imperatively the duty of obedience to their fathers, he must hold the dignity of father in the highest esteem? How venerable then is the name of father, surrounded as it is with honor by God himself!

And how honorable is fatherhood and the name of father when we look into the father's heart! How has God formed the father's heart? He made it after his own paternal heart. His heart has an infinite love for his children, an infinite desire to make them happy and to lead them to their true welfare. And such is the nature which the Lord has given to every father's heart. Such is the unconscious tendency of every uncorrupted father's heart. Find if you can a man whose heart, if God has blessed him with children, does not instinctively impel him to do everything in his power to make them happy. The world would call him an unnatural father who would not yield to this impulse. It is only in a state of barbarism that such a father is possible. Behold then the father's heart.

But who has so constituted the father's heart that when he becomes a father he is animated by these natural emotions and sentiments? It is a gift from the great heart of the heavenly Father to his image and representative on earth, a gift from the divine to the human father.

How noble does not this constitution of the father's heart make the name of father appear! God himself has made the father's heart what it is.

If the name of father is not revered, if it is sometimes despised and contemned, the reason is unfortunately found in the manner in which the high dignity is exposed by many fathers to desecration and dishonor. Without feeling or thought for the paternal dignity and the great obligations of their vocation, indifferent, nay, averse, to its duties, they disregard all those noble characteristics which distinguish the good father and retain nothing but an ugly caricature of a degenerate one.

Let us imagine a father who answers to the idea of paternal dignity. Picture to yourself a man whose life presents a model of a truly good father—who could withhold from him his profoundest admiration and respect? How highly is the name of father venerated by the children of such a father! how honored, treasured, and loved! Their whole heart is occupied in thoughts of him; absent from him, they long to be with him; his presence, his look, his word gives them delight. His memory remains uneffaceable in their hearts even after he has long rested in his grave. Is there anything more edifying, more consoling than the memory of a truly good father?

Venerable then is the name of father. It is used in all the relations and conditions of life to denote the good, the most excellent, the best. What an honorable evidence of respect for the master of a house when those of his household address him by the name of "father!" What a commendation when it is said of the head of an institution or congregation: He is a father to the institution, he is a father to the people. And can there be a greater honor for a president, king, or emperor than to be called with truth the "Father of his Country?"

Or let us look into the ecclesiastical state. When the priest exercises that most important function of his ministry in which all the care and solicitude of his heart is brought into action, and in which the faithful are accustomed to give him the highest proof of their confidence, he is called the "Father Confessor." When the priest takes especial care of a soul which he wishes to lead onward in the way of perfection he is called the "Spiritual Father." Bishop and priest who perform their high and onerous duties with particular love and care are called father of the diocese, father of the congregation. And for him who holds the highest dignity in the holy Church, for the head, the representative of Jesus Christ, no more beautiful and excellent name has been found than that of "father;" Pope means "father," and our whole heart goes out to him when we say "Our holy Father."

Honorable then is the name of father on earth. Will it not be honorable also in heaven? That mysterious sign which the elect receive in baptism and confirmation, and which the priest receives at ordination, will bear witness that they are children of God, and be their glory in heaven. Who can doubt that in like manner the dignity of father will be an everlasting glory for those who have been clothed with it here on earth?

Behold, Christian father, what thou art. The name of father is honored by both God and man, venerated on earth and glorified in heaven. Thou bearest it; it will, if thou bearest it worthily, be thy honor, thy happiness, and thy salvation in time and eternity.

Let your heart rejoice in the paternal dignity. Let the name of father be your pride. Let it be your ambition at all times and in every manner to prove yourself worthy of it.

The Father's Vocation.

His Stewardship.

FATHER is a title of honor. Names, which come from God, indicate the nature of those who bear them. The name in the present case expresses the nature of the dignity of the father, his vocation, his office.

The duty of the father, like his dignity, is from God. God made him a father when he gave him his children. Children are the gift of God. "He hath made us," says the Psalmist, "we have not made ourselves." They are God's own inheritance. "He is our God, and we are his people, sheep of his pasture." "To the Lord belongs the earth and the fulness thereof." Thy children, O father, are God's children, much more and in a higher sense than they are yours. Do you love them? He loves them still more. Do you care for them? He cares for them still more. They belong in every way much more to him than to you. He has only intrusted them to you.

Why has he intrusted them to you? Ask why he created them. The answer is: that they may grow up and become truly good men and women; that they will, for their own welfare and that of their fellow-men, correspond truly and conscientiously to their vocation, and by their life on earth gain entrance to the kingdom of God in heaven. What a task! On their fulfilment of it depends the welfare of man on earth and his happiness for all eternity.

God intrusted your children to you that you might enable them to fulfil this task; that you might assist them to become good men and women, and qualify them for their God-given vocation; that their life on earth may be devoted not only to their temporal welfare, but also to their eternal salvation.

This is the task, the charge, which the Lord has imposed on you, and if you do not perform the work which he has laid out for you, and care for your children according to the will and design of God, they will not attain their eternal destiny. They will not become good men and women if you do not do your part to that end. They will not find their vocation on earth, or correspond to its requirements, if you do not lead them to it. They will not be happy on earth, and will with difficulty gain heaven if you do not accomplish God's will in regard to them. It can be truly said: "*Thy children have been given into thy hands.*"

There are exceptions to the rule. Children to whom the father has not performed his duty, or to whom his neglect of duty and bad example have been a detriment, have become good men and women and gained salvation. God himself, by his special grace and assistance, came to their rescue, supplied what the father failed in, and compensated for the injury the unnatural father had inflicted on them. But these are exceptional and rare cases. The rule holds, that children by whom the father (and mother) have not done their duty do not become good men and women—do not, or do not in the ordinary way, obtain heaven. The decrees of the Lord are inscrutable to weak human understanding. It may be asked, Why does not the Lord do for all children what he does for a few neglected ones? A perfect knowledge of the designs of God is not always granted to us; but the fact remains that children who are neglected or corrupted by their parents remain neglected and corrupted.

Does not every man experience something of this kind? If he strives to become a good man, to find and fulfil his vocation, and to obtain temporal and eternal welfare, God will in all these efforts doubtless do the greater part by his grace and assistance. But he himself must put his own hand to the work in each particular case. When a good work is to be done, temptations to be overcome, faults to be corrected, virtues to be acquired, he must first make use of the gifts and faculties which God has given him. It is only after, and in so far as he has done this, that God ordinarily comes to his assistance by his grace to supply what is needed. But he does this only when by prayer and other pious works he is prevailed on to do so. "Help thyself," says the proverb, "and God will help thee;" that is, do your part,* and then you may hope that God will do his part if you ask him. But fail to make use of the gifts, graces, and opportunities which God has given you to free yourself from

---

*To do this man of course needs grace.

your faults, to acquire virtue, to gain eternal life, and God will not come to your assistance to supply what is needed, even if he could. You continue in your faults, remain without virtue, and are lost.

Thus it is in the mysterious decrees of the infinite wisdom, holiness and love of God. Man must—so is the decree—he must, as far as possible, be the promoter of his own happiness, as God is the cause of what he himself is and has. Man's happiness will be all the greater when it is the result of his own efforts in conjunction with the grace of God. It is in the providence of God that the welfare of one man is due in a degree to the salutary influence of others. God has so created men that they do not stand isolated from each other, but being intimately united, like the members of the body, they form a great whole. Hence, when one person wishes to attain his temporal and eternal welfare he should not be left to struggle alone, but that he may the better succeed he should be assisted by others, and he in turn should lend them a helping hand.

It is easy here to discover the gracious design of God. By this means the efforts of many make the welfare of each more certain and complete. The Lord at the same time designed, no doubt, that all should be united by a bond of holy love, so that the elect in eternity might have the happy consciousness of having assisted so many others to eternal life.

Be this as it may, it is certainly true that the welfare of the individual is determined in many ways by the salutary influence of others, and that without this influence he would gain with difficulty, or not gain at all, the desired end. To withhold help, consolation, support, advice, direction, and salutary influence from a man, is to leave him destitute of what is necessary to him to attain his destiny, and he is lost. The Lord does not interfere to supply the defect.

Well, nowhere is this in so high a degree true as in the case of children. They are in every way dependent on the salutary influence of the father and mother. If these are not careful to do their part, to make good men and women of their children, to lead them to salvation, they will all too easily yield to evil influences and be lost. Ask those unfortunates who have missed their vocation in life, or who have not complied with its requirements—living perhaps in sin and vice, and who in consequence have known no true happiness in life—ask them how this sad state of things came about.

They will almost always refer it to parents who did not do their duty by them. If it were permitted in the world beyond to ask this question of those unfortunates who are doomed to eternal perdition, how many among them would attribute the principal cause of their damnation to their parents!

Behold then, O father, your task, your mission. It is in the plan of divine wisdom that man comes into existence as a helpless infant; that his corporal life, like his spiritual and higher life, should develop from small beginnings to ever higher degrees of perfection. He therefore needs, while his twofold life is developing, support and help, a guide, a tutor, that he may reach the destined degree of perfection, as the young and tender tree needs support and care while coming to maturity.

It is for this reason that God has given parents to man, particularly during the time of his childhood and youth. As man in his infancy and youth is not able to procure what is necessary to support and prolong life the father must procure it for him. As he, ignorant and inexperienced, does not understand his vocation and welfare, the father, wiser and more experienced, must point out the right way and incline him towards it. As he, weak in body as well as in mind and will, can with difficulty continue in the right way, the father, matured by experience, confirmed in correct principles, and strong in the Christian spirit, must guide him to the right way and compel him to persevere in it.

Thus is the child, the youth, the maiden, everywhere and in all circumstances, depending on the father and mother. They almost always become what the parents make them. Can there be a greater, more important, more responsible duty than that of a father and mother?

The Qualifications of a Father.

As the Lord established this order, and committed his children in so great a degree to the care of their parents, he has also taken care to enable the parents to perform their important task. He therefore implanted in the heart of the father and mother that powerful sentiment of paternal and maternal love, that thereby they might be impelled, involuntarily, to care for their children. But that which the natural sentiment of love dictates to parents the Lord has imposed upon them as the holiest of duties. How terrible are his threats against parents who neglect their duty; how great the rewards he promises to good parents!—threats and promises which should spur them on to a more faithful performance of their duties.

God has in like manner so constituted the hearts of children that a natural tendency impels them to meet their parents half way in their efforts to instruct and direct them. Hence this sentiment of love and attachment towards father and mother in every young heart, this susceptible, credulous, open heart for all that the parents say or do, this disposition to imitate them in all things, this willingness to obey their commands,—all these dispositions God has implanted in the young heart. Here also, as in the case of the parents, God gives force to this natural tendency by precept and commandment. With what emphasis he has imposed upon children the duty of respect, love, and obedience to their parents! How has he at all times given force to his commandment by rewarding good and punishing wicked children!

While in all this the Lord had directly in view the welfare of children, which to so great an extent depends on fulfilling their duties to their parents, he also wished thereby to assist the parents the more easily to fulfil their duties to their children.

Behold then, O father, how much God relies on you fulfilling your duties to your children in compliance with his holy will! The more God has done to assure the performance of those duties the more important they should appear in your eyes.

The August Nature of a Father's Vocation.

If more were necessary to show the value and sacredness of the father's vocation attention can be directed to the sublimity of this vocation. For what could God intrust to feeble man more precious than a man?

A man! Have you ever comprehended what a man really is? A man is the most glorious work of the hand of the Lord. God called all things into being by a simple act of his holy will; he said: "Let it be made," and it was made. But when he would call man into being, the adorable persons of the most holy Trinity took council together as it were: "Let us make man!" And so "God made man in his own image, in his likeness made he him." Behold, O father, God has intrusted this glorious work of his hands to you as often as he has blessed you with children!

And how dear to him are your children! They are his children also, much more and in a higher sense than they are yours. He loves them more than you love them. "With an eternal love hath he loved them." For them he sacrificed his divine Son. And how dearly does that divine Son, the children's friend, love them. He gave up his life for them. And the Holy Ghost! He has in holy baptism taken possession of them that he may dwell and work in them as in his temple. Behold, the triune God has intrusted these most beloved children to your care, O father. You must assist him to lead these, his and thy children, to salvation. He has chosen you as his co-laborer in this holy work. O sublime calling, to be a co-laborer with God in the salvation of his children!

And what is at stake? It is a question of the well-being of your children. If only their temporal welfare was concerned how great even that would appear! How important that man even here on earth should lead a happy life! If then it were nothing more than this of what great importance it must appear to every good father. But it is a question of eternal happiness or misery. It is intrusted to the hands of the father to rescue his children from eternal perdition, and by bringing them up properly enable them to enjoy unending happiness in the world to come. Can a greater or a higher trust be imagined? It was to rescue men from perdition and lead them to eternal life that the Lord Jesus did not hesitate to accept the greatest sufferings and torments, and even to devote himself to a most ignominious death. This infinite price would have been paid for the soul of every child. O sublime task of the father in relation to his children!

Of all the duties which a father has to fulfil here on earth none can be even remotely compared to that which he owes to his children. It is, in fact, the highest occupation, the most important business of his life.

On his faithful and proper fulfilment of this duty depends, more than on anything else, his own welfare in time and in eternity. What pleasure and consolation will good parents receive, even in this world, from their sons and daughters whom they have properly brought up. Are not good children the joy, the honor, the pride, and highest happiness of their parents? But on the contrary, what sorrow, grief and affliction thoughtless parents experience from children perverted through their fault.

This is the order appointed by divine justice, a foretaste of what eternity has in store for them. How great will be the responsibility of a father who, in the hour of his judgment, must acknowledge that he mistook or neglected the highest and most important duty which God had imposed upon him on earth, and that through this neglect, want of principle, and bad example, those whom he should have brought up good men and women have grown up in evil ways—that those whom he should have lead to salvation have been lost! And, if he has not blotted out his great sin by true repentance, what a judgment, what a retribution awaits him! Is it not alone a sufficient hell for a father to be compelled to stand at that judgment seat surrounded by his own children and hear their terrible reproaches, maledictions, and imprecations?

Reflect, O father, on this, and strive with all your power to be a faithful father to your children. Who can find words to describe the rewards that await a good father in eternity? "Well done, good and faithful servant." These gracious words will be lovingly addressed by the Lord from his throne of judgment to fathers and mothers who have brought up their children properly and secured the salvation of those children whom God so dearly loves—to those fathers and mothers who assisted in realizing the yearnings of his holy heart, that the souls for whom he shed his precious blood and offered up his life might gain eternal happiness.

Yes, unspeakably great is the reward prepared for them by him who does not let a cup of water go unrewarded. Will it alone not be heaven to such a father to have his children about him in heaven, to see them eternally happy and know that he, with the help of God, was the cause of their happiness? Truly, the beautiful words of St. Augustine in reference to the elect are here realized: "Each rejoices in the happiness of the other as in his own; as many heavens as brethren;" "the father rejoices in the happiness of his children as in his own; as many heavens as children." And truly happy that father when his children bear witness before heaven that they owe their happiness, next to God, to their father and mother.

Thus everything unites to induce fathers to do their duty to their children and to fulfil that duty in the most perfect manner.

The Christian Father.

SUCH is the title of our little book. The emphasis is on the word "Christian." Truly Christian must the father be if he would perform his duty.

We have described the duties of the father's vocation. The father with the mother must so bring up the child that it may attain its destiny, which is a *Christian* destiny. Scarcely has the child been born into this world of probation when God, by his holy Church, applies to it the regenerating waters of baptism, by which it is made his child, ennobled and endowed with the highest prerogatives. He then consigns it to the care of the father and mother, his representatives, that they may bring up his and their child as becomes a child of God, and educate it to become a worthy member of the Church—a good Catholic Christian.

To bring up the child to be a Christian is the duty which God has imposed on the father (and mother). This duty can be performed only by a truly Christian father. If the father has not the true Christian spirit, if his life has not a true Christian character, if he is wanting in faith, he may do all else possible for his children, but he will not and cannot perform the life-work which God has assigned him. That which is most important of all, that on which rests their welfare in time and eternity —true Christian piety and the fear of the Lord—is denied his children, or not imparted in the proper manner.

The Christian Mother alone not Sufficient.

It may be said that "if the mother be truly Christian it will be well with the child, even if the father have not the true Christian spirit." It is true the mother, especially in the early and tender years of the child, has the greater duty of implanting in it the true Christian spirit and sentiment, and of introducing it into the Christian life. And thus a child that has not the happiness of having a good Christian father has a great recompense in a truly Christian mother. But nevertheless the training of a child in a salutary manner and in the way required by the divine will will not be accomplished if the Christian mother has not a Christian husband to put his hand to the work and assist her. The Lord has not intrusted the child to the father or to the mother, but to the father and mother together. Father and mother form a complete whole — even by nature. "Therefore," say the Scriptures, "shall a man leave his father and mother and cleave to his wife, and they shall be two in one flesh." The Lord has made this union more perfect in the holy sacrament of marriage, in which the husband and wife are united by a mysterious and indissoluble bond. They are no longer two, but one—two in one flesh.

This is in harmony with the decree of the Lord. This relationship between man and wife, so intimately and supernaturally united and blessed by the mysterious and supernatural virtue of the sacrament, should be, according to the decree of divine wisdom, the holy soil from which new men should spring up and grow to be good men, Christians, worthy members of the kingdom of God on earth and in heaven.

Neither the mother alone nor the father alone give the child life. They should then unite to lead it to its appointed goal; they should unite in the work of its Christian education. The mother may strive to give the child a good Christian training, but if the father does not assist, if he does not bring a salutary influence to bear on the child its training will scarcely be accomplished, or not in the desired manner. However much the mother may do to supply what the father fails in the reparation will always be difficult, at least without particular grace from above.

' Consider the ways of nature. The Creator has made for every plant and animal a circle of salutary influences, on which its prosperity and growth depend. If any of these influences are wanting the development of the plant or animal will be retarded.

It is the same with man. As God provides for the existence of the child, so he has ordained parents for its further development; not father or mother alone, but father and mother. The influence of both must unite in the child and act on it if the design and will of God is to be accomplished. The Creator has more fully endowed the feminine nature of the mother with those peculiar qualities and dispositions of *heart* which are required for salutary training, while he has endowed in a higher degree the masculine nature of the father with those qualities of *mind* and *will* which secure the good results of education. And as father and mother, when working together, bring the divinely appointed work of education to a successful issue, it follows that in this union of husband and wife all the influences which the great all-wise Father has ordained for a salutary education become operative.

This is true in all relations and conditions, but it is more particularly true in the Christian education of children. Christian piety takes certain shades or coloring from the peculiarities, characteristics of the man or woman, and is different as it proceeds from the father or from the mother. This shade or coloring coming from the piety of the mother will have the peculiarities of the feminine nature, heart, disposition, and therefore a certain fervor or ardor, while in the piety of the father judgment and sternness prevail, even at the expense of tenderness. Thus the more both father and mother influence the child in the right way — the mother with her amiability and gentleness, the father with his intelligence and masculine force — the more perfect will the Christian piety of the child be. But if the mother or father work alone the characteristics of the one will prevail in the child to the exclusion of the other, and the education of the child will not be effected in a desirable manner.*

---

* From this point of view it is much to be deplored when children in their early years lose their father or mother by death. How much it is to be feared that their education will be defective. May we not hope that in such cases God, the father of the widow and the orphan, will supply what may be wanting?

The Father must also be Truly Christian.

It is evident from what has been said that in the education of children the father in union with the mother must labor at this great work in order to bring it to a happy consummation. We call it a great work. And is it not? It concerns the highest and most important affair, that on which depends man's temporal and eternal welfare. Say what we may or attempt what we may, we must always return to the same truth, namely, that man can find true happiness for time and eternity only in a truly Christian life. If it is also true that, according to the rule, man comes to live a truly Christian life only when as a child he has been led to it by the united efforts of the father and mother, how great is the obligation of fathers to lead their children to a pious, Christian life! This means nothing else but to lay the foundation of their true happiness for time and eternity, and to fulfil its condition.

The greater this task of the father, and the more imperative his duty to take its fulfilment scrupulously to heart, the greater and holier appears the obligation of his being himself a true, practical Christian. For never, as we have already said, can he accomplish this great task if he is not himself animated by Christian sentiments, if he does not himself lead a true Christian life.

Let us for a moment imagine a father who does not meet these requirements. He is indifferent to God, to religion, and to virtue, lazy and negligent in prayer; he is seldom seen to pray at home. He is not fond of church-going; on Sundays a low mass is all, if even that; sermons he seldom or never hears; he goes to confession and communion very rarely, perhaps not once in the year; he never indulges in conversations about religious matters, or perhaps when he does it is only to the detriment of religion. What can be expected from all this but perversity of conduct and behavior? He is given to expressions of impatience and anger, unkindness and severity, injustice in judging others in thought and deed, hatred and enmity towards others. He is given to every kind of disorder in daily life, gluttony in eating, intemperance in drinking, insincerity, lies, and deceit. How can a child that grows up under such circumstances and influences acquire Christian sentiments or training? And what if the mother is no better, if she is given to like practices? Must not a child of such parents become almost necessarily wicked and depraved?

How many sad proofs of this our times afford! What degeneracy is frequently found among boys and girls, young men and young women! No trace of Christian piety; the greatest indifference and carelessness in religious exercises; yea, open contempt for religion—doubt and unbelief. And what a moral degeneracy this implies! What a beginning for the happiness of life! What a sacrifice to sin and excess! Most sad and affecting, but not surprising when we see how fathers and mothers conduct themselves. Unhappy children who do not receive from those whom God has constituted their leaders and guides to salvation the essential conditions of it—piety and the fear of God. What a terrible account must such parents render!

But let us suppose that a child whose father acts in the manner just described has yet a good mother, and receives from her a good Christian training. In this supposition the efficiency of the mother, which is so essential, still lacks the complement of the father's co-operation, and the consequence is that the Christian training of the child is not successfully accomplished. It is in no way satisfactory. And besides, while such a father would not second the mother in her efforts, he would in many ways interrupt, hinder, and check her efficiency, or positively exert an injurious influence on the child—what she builds up he pulls down.

All depends on the child, from infancy up, receiving salutary, religious impressions at home; that religion and virtue appear to it the most important and honorable; that it be accustomed to see and judge everything in the light of the faith; that it learn from the faith how to live. All this may be accomplished by the efforts of a good mother, and yet it will not be perfect if the child perceives that what the mother represents as worthy and important is a matter of indifference to the father; that he concerns himself little about it, and seldom or never speaks of it. And how will it be if the child observes that the father is not only indifferent to the salutary efforts of the mother, but actually averse to them? And what if it hears words and speeches expressing this aversion?

Or it is a question of leading the child to a Christian life. The mother devotes herself to it. Instructing, animating, directing by word and example, she seeks early to accustom the child to morning and evening prayer, to visit the church, to hear the word of God, and at proper times to receive the sacraments; she warns it against sin and leads it to overcome it; she strives to accustom it to the practice of the Christian virtues. But O how wickedly may the results of her admirable efforts be destroyed by the father! Or can we expect that the child will have these Christian efforts and practices duly impressed on its heart if it observes little or nothing of them in its father, or that he is indifferent or averse to them?

The effect of the father's indifference or aversion to them will work all the worse on account of the child's natural disposition to imitate especially the father, and on account of the greater authority and influence which the father exercises over the child as it grows up. Only too easily, therefore, will the child by degrees, and despite all the guidance and instruction of the mother, become negligent in prayer if it never sees the father pray, or if it sees him make little of it. The father is negligent in attending church and acts as if it were of no consequence; what wonder if the child, little by little, becomes equally negligent? The father avoids hearing the Word of God, going out at the sermon; the son follows him down the aisle and out. Why do children of such a household receive so seldom the sacraments while others are so zealous in receiving them? Because they have seen and followed the example of their father. It is an old proverb: Example draws. The *words* of the mother may urge and exhort, but the *example* of the father draws the children and is imitated by them.

So will the shame of certain sins and perverse actions by degrees die out in the child if it observes these sins and actions in the father, and it will soon betake itself to them. And the Christian virtues—is it probable that a child will persevere in the practice of them if it does not see the father practise them?

Understand it well, you fathers, and think how great and irreparable is the injury you inflict on your children when you do not persevere in Christian sentiment and lead a truly Christian life. Through your fault there remains lacking that on which more than all else depends the welfare of your children and without which they cannot secure their salvation. Yea, through your wicked example you directly cause their ruin. How will you account on the last day to him who gave you these children—his children? What a fearful judgment awaits you—how terrible will your punishment be!

The Importance of this Obligation.

Of all the many strong motives to a Christian life which our holy faith affords to every one, the strongest to a father is love and regard for his children. It is one of his holiest duties, one on which his salvation intimately depends, to bring up his children in piety and the fear of God; and this he cannot do unless he himself be confirmed in piety and the fear of God. The more children God has given him the more obligations he has to practice a truly Christian life.

Fortunate for the child whose father fulfils these obligations, whose father, in union with the mother, is active in the infinitely important work of his religious and moral training. The salutary influence which the pious mother exercises to this end is greatly increased by the fact that the father is imbued with piety and the fear of the Lord. Then all that the child hears, sees, or learns is Christian, in accord with the teachings and precepts of our holy faith. The Church, her teachings, her precepts, her customs, and the virtues of a Christian life become to the child more and more venerable and holy, for they are holy to the father and mother. That which is opposed to these holy teachings, precepts, and customs become to it more and more detestable, and it shuns and avoids it, for father and mother do the same. From early youth it will become a second nature to it to think, reflect, judge, speak, and act in a Christian manner, to perform the exercises of a Christian life faithfully and zealously, and to practise the Christian virtues; for father and mother do so, and their life is its mirror. Their example brings powerfully into action that propensity to imitate which God has implanted in its nature. Yes, it would be astonishing if a child that has a truly Christian father and mother would not be brave and good, instructed and happy. Happy child, therefore, that has such a father and such a mother.

It is one of the greatest graces for a child to have a good mother, but this grace is perfected and completed only when with this mother it has a good father. By a good mother the proper bringing up of the child is in a high degree assured, but still more is it assured when a truly Christian father puts his hand to the work and assists the mother in her holy efforts.

O fathers, who will give us the power to make you understand how much depends on your being Christian fathers?

The Model Christian Father.

WE have thus far given several features of this model; we will now, on account of its great importance, present them in a more complete manner.

The Sketch.*

Who is a Christian father? In general the answer is very simple. A father is a Christian father when he is a good (Catholic) Christian. But who is a good Catholic Christian? Every one knows the answer. He is a Catholic Christian who, co-operating with the grace of faith, not only accepts and firmly holds the doctrines taught by our holy religion, but whose thoughts, words, acts, and whole life are regu-

---

* Before the painter enters on the execution of a picture he makes the general outlines of it; he makes a sketch.

lated by the doctrines and precepts of the faith.

To be a Catholic Christian it is not enough to *know* the teachings of our holy religion and *believe* them, a man must make those teachings operative in his life; he must publicly profess them in word and act, and make manifest by his public conduct that he is a Catholic Christian.

Thus should every one act, whether a father or not. It is the condition of being in reality a Catholic Christian, and not being merely a so-called one; it is a condition of salvation. But the father is bound more imperatively in this matter on account of his children, because it is a condition without which the children cannot become good Catholic Christians. He is a truly Christian father who so acts and lives. The Christian father has certain parental duties to fulfil towards his children, but as a good Christian he would perform these duties for his own sake, for these particular duties belong also to the duties of the Christian faith and are among the holiest of them.

Here is another outline of the sketch: A father in whom the picture of a good Christian father is presented to the eyes of his children is one in whom they can see what a Catholic Christian is, how he judges, what he loves, what he shuns, how he speaks, how silent, what he avoids, what he does, and how he does it.

Does it not appear clearly from this what it signifies to be a truly Christian father? From the example of such a father a twofold advantage arises; we only indicate it here:

First, the children learn in the simplest manner their holy religion, its teachings and precepts, and the various relations of a right Christian life. These are daily presented to their eyes in a series of living pictures by their father and mother. How much better does a child understand this practical application of Christian teaching than it comprehends bald and naked instruction? It is easier to see and imitate than it is to understand, easier to *show* how to act than *tell* how to act. This fact is appreciated even in our schools, where pictures are made use of that the child may see with its eyes what it is taught by words, and by this means it understands its lesson much easier and better.

Secondly, the children, on the supposition that the parents not only know and believe the Christian religion, but also practise it, have before their eyes the acts and lives of the father and mother, and will thereby be lead, in a simpler and better way, to Christian practice and life than they could be by mere verbal teaching. How much more forcibly are we all, but particularly children, impressed by what is daily set before us than by mere verbal instruction. And here it must be observed that children have a strong inclination to imitate what they observe in their father and mother. This inclination or impulse was put into their hearts by God himself.

Therefore, we repeat, it would be surprising if a child that has before its eyes, in its father and mother, a picture of a good Catholic Christian, would not also become a good Catholic Christian.

While writing this the consciousness arises in our heart most vividly and strikingly how exceedingly important it is for a father to be a good Christian; and the more we have the sad knowledge that many are not Christians the more we are here impelled, before giving the details of the father's picture, to preface it with a warning.

A Word to the Heart of the Father.

You love your children. The wish to see them happy has grown with your heart. We therefore repeat, your wish will never be realized if you do not bring them up good Christians—*never*. Be assured if you do not bring them up good Christians you place a cause that will destroy their happiness, a cause that will bring them to eternal misery. You must make your children good Christians if you wish to secure their welfare.

Again, your desire for the happiness of your children will never be realized if you yourself are not a good Catholic Christian—*never*. Can a tradesman who does not practise his trade or who does not understand it instruct an apprentice to become a master of the trade? Can you teach a young man to be the master of an art if you are ignorant of it yourself? Much less can a father bring up his children to be good Christians if he is not one himself.

Here is the way it stands with you.

You should make your children happy, and you wish to do so from your innermost heart; you cannot make them happy if you do not see to it that they grow up good Christians; and you cannot do this if you yourself are not a good Christian, or if you do not strive earnestly to be one. That is the way it stands, whether you believe it or not; whether you forget it or not, it does not alter the case; *so it is*, and *so it remains;* the happiness of your children depends on your being a good Catholic Christian.

But are you? Alas, no! An evil, sinful youth lies behind you—full of levity, indiscretion, and sin. Your past life has warred against your Christian heart, against your conscience, and perhaps even against your faith. You have thrown yourself into the arms of sin, impurity, and intemperance. You have had the misfortune of intercourse with dissolute young people. You were perhaps a soldier in our late war, and from your companions you acquired many bad habits. The grand campaigns you have gone through, and of which with reason you are proud, have perhaps loosened your conscience and weakened your fervor. Add to this the bad books and bad newspapers that carry you away, drifting like a straw in the tide. O, how have these writings which you have devoured filled your soul and your life with poison!

Such then is your life. Besides, through an excess of worldly striving, you have been estranged from God—given to sins, and many even of the worst kind. They still weigh on your conscience all too heavily; for you have never seriously undertaken by that repentance and confession, which such a life makes necessary, to reconcile yourself with God, and you stand before him in disgrace.

And what of your faith? Has it not

been weakened by all those sinful excesses of your life, by dissolute and frivolous conversations and bad examples, by all the bad books and papers you have read?

But if you are not as yet so far gone, how is it with your Christianity? How is it that everything that concerns God, religion, and your soul's salvation is so far from you, so strange to you, and why are you so indifferent about these things? You do not pray, or your prayer is an idle repetition of memorized formulas. You do not love the Church or divine service; how reluctantly you go to church, how seldom, and then without heartfelt sympathy or participation. As for confession and communion, you have an aversion to them and avoid them as much as possible. And when you do go, alas! the pen refuses to give full expression to the thoughts. And your daily life, how full of disorder, irregularity, perverse-

The Model Christian Father. 69

ness, and sins of many kinds—of anger and impatience, severity and unkindness to wife, children, and household. Add to this intemperance in eating and drinking, the violation of holy purity; and is there not also dishonesty, lies, and frauds in business and traffic, and unjust possession of property?

And you are a father! Poor children who have such a father! Who will bring you up good Catholic Christians? And yet without this you will never be happy. Will it be otherwise with you, will you in time be better than your father? O, how much it is to be feared that his example will have more influence over your young hearts than all the instruction which you may elsewhere receive. With bleeding heart we see it coming, you will also in time follow in the wicked footsteps of your father, you also will give yourselves up to frivolities and sin, you also will lead an unchristian life and lose your faith. You will be unhappy. Poor children!

O father, does not the impending fate of your children move you?

Then have mercy! Become what you must be to make them happy, become what thus far you have not been, *from this time forth become a good father*.

Whatever your past life may have been, howsoever full of sin and evil it may be at present, now at least *will* earnestly, *will* to become a good Christian father. Look upon your children and say to yourself: "They can never be truly happy if I do not become a good Christian father." Then may your love for your children and your desire for their happiness develop its full power in your heart and bring you to the firm resolution: "Yes, I will henceforth be a good father."

Be assured such a resolution will cause joy in heaven. The great Father in heaven will meet such a resolution with mercy and grace. Be assured that as he has the salvation of your children and your own so much at heart, and as he desires that you become a good Christian father, he is disposed and prepared to exercise mercy towards you and to forgive your sins if you appeal to him with an humble and contrite heart. He is ready to assist you with every grace that you may become a good Christian father. Surely, if there is joy in heaven over one sinner who does penance, there will be a twofold joy over a father who does penance and resolves to become a good Christian father; yes, as many rejoicings as he has children; yes, as he may have children's children. His reformation is their deliverance, his salvation their salvation. Up, then, and henceforth *be a good Christian father*.

On this your own welfare for time and eternity depends. Or say, have you then in all your former acts and inclinations ever found what your heart desired? Come, acknowledge. If you will testify to the truth and lay open the inmost recesses of your soul you must confess that you never found true peace of soul in all your former unchristian life.

Christian faith and Christian life—that is the divinely appointed way of salvation for time and eternity. In it, and only in it, is found peace and true happiness in this life and in the next. In it "you will find rest for your souls." Outside of it, and in wandering from it in sin and perversity, lies the loss of true peace and happiness; yes, still more, their destruction, woe, distress, suffering, ruin. "Tribulation and distress in the soul of every one who does evil."

You must then be a true Christian in order to be happy yourself, and in order to make your children happy. If you are a good Christian you will also be a good father and secure the happiness of your children, for you will not only perform your paternal duties to them, but you will also present to them by the course of your life a picture of a good Christian father, and thereby with the grace of God make sure that they also will become good Christians and be happy; for every true, good Christian is happy.

The Full Picture.

Let us now complete the picture of such a Christian father in its individual traits as they appear to the eyes of the children.

From his conversation, actions, and conduct it is evident that he is a true son of the holy Catholic Church; that all her teachings, precepts, and customs are holy in his eyes; that he is firm in the Catholic faith, and ready, when occasion requires, to declare it without reserve.

The children see the days of fasting and abstinence observed by their father; they see him make with reverence the sign of the cross; they see him revere things blessed by the Church; he disdains not to adorn his house with religious pictures. He is—they see it daily—given to prayer. He offers prayer before and after meals; there is prayer morning and evening and on many other occasions. The Sundays and feast-days are observed with reverence; there is no work except what is necessary. He loves to spend some time in church, not merely at a low mass, but at high mass, preaching, and vespers. He takes pleasure in conversing at home, to speak of the solemnities of the Church and what has been said in the sermon. He takes an interest in the Church and her fortunes, in her head, the holy father, and in everything that concerns her, and likes to speak of all these things; the children hear them from his lips and are edified; he explains to them the affairs and occurrences of the day and gives them salutary instructions, explanations, and suggestions. They see him going more than once a year to confession and communion, and with what holy earnestness he performs these duties.

In his house the priests receive due honor and respect; the children see and remark that the father treats them according to their dignity and holds their office in honor. The same is the case with the teachers; the same with the civil authorities, according to the maxim "Honor to whom honor is due."

The family has its history; events take place, happy or otherwise, and they receive the consecration of the Church. Everything is begun with God—according to its importance with greater or less solicitude—with prayer, devotion, solemnity.

Thus everything in the life of the

family receives in the consecration of the Church a religious coloring, not in an ostentatious, pharisaical way, but in a simple manner and according to the Catholic spirit.

With this religious forming and Catholic coloring of the family's life goes hand in hand the corresponding moral tendency. The whole life is Catholic in thought, word, and work.

Before all there is the relation of the father to the mother, to the children, and to the other members of the household. A Christian relationship of love, concord and peace produces gentleness, tranquillity, and composure, savored by mutual service and complaisance. And if now and then, through human weakness, misunderstandings occur, they are but light clouds which momentarily overshadow the clear rays of the sun of peace. All this is beautifully expressed in the words of the Psalmist: "Behold how good and how pleasant it is for brethren to dwell together in unity; it is like the precious ointment on the head, that ran down upon the beard, the beard of Aaron; which ran down the skirt of his garment, as the dew of Hermon, or that which descended upon Mount Sion." *

Charity, that distinguishing mark of the true Christian, is here domestic; no one is exempt from it. The father has—the children constantly see new proofs of it—he has a heart for all; therefore no uncharitable talk about others, no fault-finding, no calumny, no detraction or slander; away with jealousy and envy, dislike, hatred, and revenge; away with mortifying or injuring neighbors. As far as in him lies such a father realizes the words of the Apostle: "Follow peace with all men."

Again, it belongs to the order of the house to be obliging and render service

---

* Psalm cxxxii. 1-3.

to our neighbors and fellow-men; the poor and needy find an attentive ear and a heart willing to afford all possible assistance. Need it be added that in this house offences against Christian propriety, intemperance and gluttony are unknown—not tolerated.

To conclude: the father—such was our supposition—is a good Catholic Christian, and for that reason a good father. The mother is a truly Christian mother. What follows? The spirit which animates the father and mother by degrees pervades the whole house; this spirit nourishes in both parents and children those precious fruits which the Apostle calls the fruits of the Holy Ghost. "They are," he says, " charity, joy, peace, patience, benignity, goodness, longanimity, mildness, faith, modesty, continency, chastity."

They fill the whole house with their sweet fragrance and rejoice the heart with their grateful savor; they promote the increase of the Christian spirit and the growth of every virtue in the hearts and lives of the children; they are a sweet savor before the Lord, and his grace rules over such a house and its inmates.

Happy children who grow up in such a house! Happy children who have such a father!

How may this Picture be Realized?

But do we not expect too much of the father—the man? Is not the piety, described in the foregoing picture, the business of the mother—the woman—and not to be required of the man?

Nothing is farther from our intention than to require from the father anything that is impossible to him, or only possible at the expense of his masculine character. We require nothing more of him than what his character as a Christian demands of him as a father, nothing that would wound his masculine character, nothing that he, as a man, could be ashamed of; on the contrary, what we require of him would the more ennoble his masculine nature and make him what God designed he should be—a true man.

What, then, is required of a man in order to be a good Christian father? First and most important, he must be devout; he must accept and hold the doctrines of our holy religion as taught by the Church, and the truths which God has revealed. What is there here unworthy of a man or impossible to him? Can we imagine that any one of sufficient intelligence who calmly examines religion could fail to accept it as true? How, then, has it happened that in all times men who have made themselves conspicuous by their talents and wisdom, and who had the best opportunities to examine and weigh the reasons for and against, have found no reason to doubt the doctrines of our holy religion, but on the contrary have embraced them with devout confidence and joy? It is true there are and always have been many conspicuous for their intelligence and ability, who felt themselves justified in rejecting the faith ; but let us be assured, it was not because of their intelligence or because they had found nothing in the faith, it was because by the misuse of their talents and their sinful degeneracy they had lost the sense of the teachings of faith as well as the grace of faith.

What is required of a Christian father? He is required to practice certain exercises of the Christian life ; he is required, in proportion to his personal, domestic, and other circumstances, to devote some time to prayer, to attendance at divine service, to receiving the sacraments, and to afford his children the example of a faithful Catholic life.

What is there in this unworthy of or

unbecoming a man? We have admitted that all these are not to be done precisely as the mother performs them, although that, according to circumstances, is in order and to be recommended; but we can always mitigate these requirements in the supposed cases without fearing that the father will thereby suffer in his Christian character. In the duties referred to let the father always maintain his masculine character, but in the right way. But to understand how it can be in any way unworthy of a father to practise those exercises which the spirit of religion and the precepts of the Church impose on him, or that it would injure his masculine dignity, surpasses our comprehension. Unfortunately, the number of those fathers who are zealous in this matter is not so very large; but there is no doubt that among those who belong to this number are to be found the genuine, true men. Who would dare to question the manhood of the leaders of the Centre in the chamber of deputies at Berlin? The whole Catholic world looks upon them as models of true manhood; even their opponents admit it. Well, then, it is known that they are true and devout members of the Church; that they are particularly zealous in the practice of those pious exercises.* Or is it impossible for a man, according to his condition in life, to prove himself a good Christian father by a proper zeal in these religious exercises? He who asserts this is directly refuted by the fact that there are, and always have been, in all classes and conditions of life, fathers who have practised these exercises and fulfilled all the requirements of their Christian

---

* One of the best of them, after the death of his wife, and as long as her remains were unburied, went every morning to holy communion, in order to obtain consolation and strength in his great affliction.

and paternal vocation. Why should it be impossible to a father? It is the same as to say that it is impossible to lead a Christian life. They are the same. It may, we admit, be sometimes difficult to a father, and require some effort, perseverance, and sacrifice. But he who on that account thinks himself justified in giving up, renounces that future reward which can be obtained only by great effort. "The kingdom of heaven suffers violence, and the violent alone bear it away."

Lastly, what is required of a Christian father? It is required that he scrupulously avoid that which our holy faith condemns and forbids; that he study to fulfil the duties of a Christian life, and practise virtue. This every Christian must do if he wishes to work out his salvation. But if a father does this he is, from the fact, a good Christian father, and he does only what, as a Christian, he must do. Is this not possible to him? Is it, then, not possible for him to be a good Christian? Who, then, can excuse himself? who plead impossibility?

But Let Us be Just.

We must insist that every father should be a truly Christian father. To say that the piety which is required of a father is not practicable or becoming in a man is to contend against reason and faith.

It cannot, however, be denied that the father, in the practice of the piety required of him, meets very often with many difficulties. We have in view here not those general difficulties which are met with in the Christian life at all times, we speak here of the particular difficulties which, more or less, meet the father. They are found partly in his masculine nature and partly in the particular duties and circumstances of his life.

While the mother is led to the practice of piety by her natural inclination, with the father this is much seldomer the case. He is governed more by cold reason. He does from calculation and a sense of duty what the mother does from impulse and inclination. His way is certainly the more difficult. He does not generally in the practice of a Christian life find so much satisfaction as the mother experiences; this again makes it more difficult for him. He is generally more occupied in the labors and cares of life; it is therefore often difficult enough for him to persevere in his devotion to God, to maintain a sense of higher things and the fervor of a Christian life. To this it must be added that the life of the man is generally more subject to dangers and temptations of many kinds than that of the mother in her more limited and secluded sphere. Will his exposed life not lead him too much to the enjoyment of pleasures, to unseasonable visits to public houses, to intemperance in drinking, to offences against Christian justice, to offences against purity? And then the danger to his faith! These dangers consist in the undue preponderance of mere intellect, and still more in the injurious influence which the unavoidable intercourse with men indifferent in the faith or given to unbelief exercises over him; add to this the reading of bad books, newspapers, and other writings.

All these are circumstances which are calculated to lead men by degrees to become indifferent to God and careless in religious exercises, and to induce them to give themselves up to worldly pursuits, worldly-mindedness, perverseness and sins of all kinds, by which their faith is injured or lost. What, then, is to be done?

The Picture Finished.

Can all these difficulties and dangers be overcome? We reply: There are, thank God, very many fathers who, although exposed to these difficulties and dangers, are nevertheless very good Christians. It comes ever and always to this: If you wish to lead a Christian life you must have a firm, determined, good will; then with the grace of God you can overcome danger and temptation. What, then, is to be done?

Do not multiply difficulties without necessity.

No doubt necessity and unavoidable circumstances, as work, business, cares, and diversions, leave many a father little time to instruct his children as he would wish to instruct them. This is so much to be deplored that we may hope in such cases the Lord himself by his grace will supply to the children what the father, through no fault of his own, fails to give them.

But we cannot reasonably entertain this hope if the father overloads himself with work or business without weighty reason, or through ambition or an inordinate desire of gain. Such an unreasonable devotion to the world and worldly affairs will work evil to himself; it will destroy his soul and cause the most important work of his life—the good education of his children—to be neglected, or not performed in a proper manner.

The conscientious father is careful, and he must be, to confine his work or business to moderate limits, corresponding to his necessities and circumstances.

Is this not done in all important matters? If a man has an undertaking involving important consequences he seeks to lay aside or defer everything that may hinder its success or render it doubtful; he further makes every arrangement that may conduce to its success. And as long as he has it at heart it will, to a certain extent, succeed. But is there any business or undertaking that can be compared, even remotely, in importance and consequences to the task of the father? In this case, then, we have a right to expect the same, yes, more care and attention, to do everything to insure success.

What is it that most interests those who are overburdened with business or work? Is it not the welfare of their children? It is for them they acquire, for them they persevere in work; they have in view their support, advancement, and temporal welfare. Well, then, if they have so much at heart the temporal welfare of their children should they not have more at heart their eternal happiness? Is it just to them to so devote yourself to their temporal welfare that you become incapable of doing anything for their eternal happiness? Is this not cruelty to them? It most certainly is. When you devote yourself so entirely to worldly occupations you have no time to attend properly to their salvation.

Christian father, observe moderation in your temporal occupations. Do not throw yourself entirely into worldly affairs. Do not entangle yourself in every undertaking. Take care to so regulate your affairs and occupations that you will still have time to devote to your children; that you will have leisure to do for them that which will aid yourself to make progress in the spiritual life, so that you may be a truly Christian father. Take care that in all your various occupations you will pay proper and due attention to your daily prayers, to divine service, to frequenting the holy sacraments, and to devoting yourself to other works of Christian piety.

Avoid Danger.

I. Dangers Against Faith.

The greatest danger for every Christian, and therefore for every Christian father, is to be found in those things which endanger or tend to undermine his faith. Faith is the foundation of all Christian life, and consequently a necessary condition of true happiness for man in time and eternity. How wretched is the life of man here on earth without faith! How terrible his anticipations of eternity! "He that believeth not shall be condemned," says the Lord, and his word is truth.

The greatest misfortune for man, therefore, is to suffer shipwreck of his faith; the greatest sin when he breaks allegiance to faith and Church. And if such a misfortune befalls a father the foundation of a Christian education is swept away from under the feet of his children, and thus the essential condition of their true welfare is made impossible for time and eternity. Oh, unspeakable misfortune to a family when the father has lost his faith or even wavers in it!

And yet how great is the danger which besets a father in these evil days, when he is compelled to associate daily and hourly with men who waver in their faith, who have become unbelievers, who mock at religion and faith, and make the teachings and practices of the holy Church a laughing stock; when he reads books written by unbelieving and immoral men and replete with their sentiments; when he takes periodicals and papers which never tire in ridiculing the holy Church and her teachings; and when, in addition to all this, he leads that sensual and idle life which conduces to gluttony and intemperance. In fact, it would almost require a miracle to preserve faith under such circumstances, for there are so many dangerous paths leading to sin and licentiousness which are so many highways to infidelity.

O Christian father, remember your children, and while you are fondly thinking of them consider what a precious treasure faith is to you, their father. Faith is indeed the most necessary condition for your children to receive that which God wills they should obtain through you, namely, the gift of true Christian sentiments and a life corresponding to them. Guard therefore carefully a treasure in which you and your children will find, in the strict sense of the word, every blessing for time and eternity. Avoid as far as possible everything that may endanger your faith. Avoid all intimate intercourse with persons who have no faith, or not the true faith. Reject with disdain every book, paper, or periodical which contains attacks against the Church, religion, and good morals.

Do not imagine that all this will **not**

or cannot injure you. If you are hesitating in your faith it will positively do you harm and surely destroy your faith. But even if you are firm in your faith such intercourse and such readings will do you injury. They will gradually but surely have the same effect on the life of your soul that the cold north wind has on nature in spring; its growth is checked, buds and blossoms are blighted, and many a tree in full bloom is robbed of its promised fruit.

Oh, how many who were once firm in the faith have lost it in this manner! May we not think that many of those who have fallen away would not have done so if they had practised their religion and avoided reading bad books and newspapers? They, too, thought it would not hurt them; but they gradually inhaled the poison which brought on death. Therefore, O Christian father, take warning!

II. On Visiting Public Houses.

We need scarcely remark that in mentioning public houses among things to be avoided it is not our intention to condemn visits to decent and proper public houses. What fault can after all be found with a father who, visiting a decent public house, takes a moderate glass with his friends, and thus finds that recreation and rest which he may need after the toils and fatigue of the day? It is only excess in this point that deserves blame and censure, and against which one should be on one's guard. Not the least among the unfavorable effects of visiting public houses is the fact that the father loses more or less that spirit of piety and the fear of the Lord which is of the greatest importance to his children.

It is perhaps especially on Sunday that such unseasonable recreation is taken, and where then shall we look for the blessing and sanctity of that day, on which the existence and progress of the spiritual life depends in so high a degree? Or what can remain of the fruits of the Sunday when a great part of the forenoon, and still a greater part of the afternoon until late in the night, is wasted in a tavern? In this way all religious sentiment and life is rendered void, or injured by the mischievous atmosphere which is generally found there. What wonder then that the spiritual life, which finds little or no nourishment during the week, dies out by degrees. No one who understands the matter can doubt that the principal reason of the religious and moral depravity of many is to be found in a neglect to observe the Sunday properly. There is nothing so detrimental to a proper observance of the Sunday as spending the time in a tavern.*

---

* As we have the father in view here, how greatly does not a disorderly tavern life lessen the blessings of the Sunday for his household,

But aside from the Sunday. If a man spends the most of his time in the tavern or public house the true Christian spirit cannot abide in him. It is a dangerous and slippery road, leading by degrees to the fatal vice of drunkenness; for by repeated and prolonged visits to the tavern you acquire an inclination and passion for drinking. The fact that one cannot refrain from visiting the tavern at certain times indicates a

---

for his children! The Sunday cannot long appear to them a holy and sacred day when experience teaches them that it is precisely on this day that the father is not to be found at home; that it is on Sunday he passes the greater part of his time in the tavern, and when he comes home in the evening, or perhaps late at night, they notice that he is under the influence of liquor, or perhaps even drunk. This bad example counteracts the good impressions which that sacred day is so well calculated to impress on their minds. How easily could that day be made the occasion of true Christian joy and recreation, when father, mother, and children, seated about the dinner or supper-table (which is better supplied on Sunday

passion unworthy of a Christian and injurious to piety. The impressions received at such places are not calculated to aid you in acquiring pious sentiments; on the contrary, all you see, hear, and do, the conversation, the reading, the singing, etc., is disadvantageous to you, and its continued repetition will more and more estrange your heart from a Christian habit of life. And when, as is frequently the

---

than other days), exchange their thoughts and views, and socially and pleasantly entertain each other. The rest from servile work, the feeling that it is an extraordinary day, conduces to this end. And then how beneficial and salutary is not such a scene in the family life. Now all this vanishes when the father spends the time in the tavern and when he shows the disgusting signs of intemperance. Sunday evenings are tedious, tiresome, and unpleasant, for the father is not there; and the poor mother cannot be very happy, expecting as she does the husband to return late, and who knows in what condition? Poor wife, poor children! It is very sad.

case in large places, every day that God gives you is spent in the tavern, how can Christian piety live and flourish?

Now, Christian father, what has been your habit in this matter? You will find perhaps that you are not guiltless of some excess or other in this regard. We therefore counsel you to retrace your steps and enter upon the path that leads to Christian moderation and regularity. If you do not it is greatly to be feared that you will render yourself unfit to fulfil one of the holiest obligations towards your children.

Far be it from us to deny you proper and necessary recreation; on the contrary, we would encourage you to enjoy it, but of course under certain conditions. Reflect for a moment. Ask yourself if the recreation which you need can be found only in the tavern. There are many men in the same circumstances as you are who seldom or never visit the tavern, and yet they are contented and enjoy life. Experience teaches that he who seeks recreation exclusively in the tavern does not taste the true joys of life. If you had learned and accustomed yourself to seek amusement and recreation in your own family circle, in the society of your wife and children, or in the company of select friends and acquaintances, you would find pleasures more refreshing and beneficial than can be found in the atmosphere of the promiscuous company to be met with at the tavern.

But we do not intend to argue the question here. We admit that after all it is your own business; that the visit to a decent public house and the company found there is not so easily dispensed with. If you think so, very well; but observe discretion and moderation. This is not a matter of opinion, it is an obligation. It is your duty to see to it that your visits to the tavern do not become a passion, a habit, or a necessity; in a word, that you do not become a slave. You must give up the daily visits and by degrees habituate yourself to stay at home. Can you not do this? If not, your passion is of a very serious nature, and you may well ask if your conduct is not disgraceful to yourself and to those whom you love.

Be careful not to idle away your time in the tavern, day or night. Does it not occur to you that to pass hour after hour thus is unbecoming and disgraceful? It is bad enough for any man, but it is especially bad for the father of a family to have the habit of staying out late at night in such places. Nothing is so destructive of true Christian morality.

But this advice is useless unless you resolve to lay down certain fixed rules for yourself on this point, rules from which you will not deviate unless for very grave reasons. The first rule refers to time. It is this: Remain *only so long and no longer; never pass the appointed time—never; go home at a fixed hour* and permit nothing to detain you beyond that time.

As to drinking, let it be so much and *no more! Never any more under any circumstances whatever.* You may say this is impossible—very hard to do. It is hard of course to keep your resolution in many cases, particularly if the disorderly life above described has become a habit; but it is not impossible. Remember, dear friend, how often you have overcome even greater difficulties when you were convinced that it had to be done and that it was for your own good.

Now it is not only your own welfare that is here at stake, but also that of your children. We have explained above how a life such as you have been leading will destroy in you all sentiment of religion, deprive your children of the advantages of a Christian education, and ruin you and them. It is your duty to reform your life; your own welfare and that of your children depend on it. It requires earnestness and fixedness of purpose; those alone succeed who are earnest and persevering.

III. Do not Fail to Practise the Christian Life.

This is an essential condition for the education of children. The father must therefore be a Christian and lead a truly Christian life. As there is so much at stake, the father should avoid everything that might make the acquisition and possession of Christian piety difficult

But, even with the best intentions, this cannot be done so thoroughly that there will not remain danger and difficulty for the father. It is therefore necessary to use the proper means to strengthen and increase the spirit of Christian piety in the father's heart, so that he may overcome all difficulties and dangers. These means, so necessary for all conditions of life, are well known; it will be proper, however, and even necessary to mention them here for the benefit of fathers, and to explain how and why the faithful and fervent use of these means is of more than ordinary importance.

1. *In what does the Christian Life consist?*

The first means is to frequently ask yourself the above question. A man must have an interest in a thing before he will take an interest in it. Who will interest himself in a matter that he cares nothing about? If a father cares nothing about piety and the fear of the Lord he will trouble himself very little about the means of acquiring them, and will care little about them.

All depends on this, that a man be animated by the spirit of true piety and the fear of the Lord. This is the only task imposed on man by God. All other means should be used to attain this great object. This is according to the intention and will of God. When this short life has passed away and the future taken its place everything that was dear to man's heart in this world will have lost its importance forever. One thing alone will retain its value, and that is true piety and the fear of the Lord. They who have practised these faithfully will be eternally happy, while they who did not will be eternally miserable.

And having a father in view we must not forget his children; according as he practises or neglects the above virtues they will follow in his footsteps, and consequently they will be eternally happy or miserable with him.

Of how great importance then is it

not for a father to be actuated by sincere Christian piety and the fear of the Lord. Everything depends on this. *It is a question of his and his children's temporal and eternal welfare.*

This, Christian father, I shall often recall to your mind, in order that you may not forget yourself amid the anxieties and distractions of life. Interrogate yourself frequently and say: What is my purpose, my object, in all my temporal affairs, in my work, business, and cares? What other purpose could I have in striving to gain this good or to avoid that evil but my own welfare and that of my children? Now there is nothing so intimately connected with my welfare and that of my children as the practice of the virtue of piety and the fear of the Lord; nothing that can bring such great evils on me and my children as the neglect of this exercise by indifference and sin.

Now what inference should you draw

from all this? "It is right and just that nothing should be so near to my heart as the faithful and persevering exercise of piety and the fear of God."

What is necessary to obtain this? The answer will show us the other means.

2. *Prayer.*

Say especially your morning and evening prayers. This must be an invariable rule. He who does not recite at least a short prayer mornings and evenings shows that if the spiritual life is not totally extinct in him it is at least in a decaying condition. Now in consequence of this neglect the spiritual life will surely decay as a man is carried away by worldly cares and gives himself up to sin. Or must he not lose all sense of higher things when he does not recall to mind the eternal truths and his high destiny at least at the beginning and end of the day? And then his poverty of grace! Our holy faith teaches us that man is incapable of avoiding sin without the divine assistance, incapable of fulfilling the obligations which he must fulfil in order to be saved. In the ordinary course of divine providence man will only receive God's helping grace when he asks for it in a proper manner. For this reason every Christian should, particularly in the morning, beseech of the Lord the grace that he needs to overcome all temptations during the day, to live and to act during that day according to his divine pleasure. If he does not pray he may very likely lack that grace, and what then will be the consequence? He will waver in temptation, stagger and fall; that day will be void of works pleasing to God and meritorious for eternity; that day, instead of being the means of bringing him near to God, may bring him nearer to hell. And what shall we say if he habitually neglects his prayers? Now if it be true, as we have shown above, that men and fathers are in greater danger of being carried away by temporal affairs, that they are assailed more frequently and by stronger temptations, is not morning and evening prayer a double necessity to them? There can be no doubt that the omission and neglect of this simple and easy exercise is the principal cause why men—fathers—are imbued with so little of the Christian spirit and true piety, to the great injury of their children.

We have called the punctual observance of the morning and evening devotions a simple and easy task. Is it not? On rising, while dressing, or on your knees, or standing if you choose, you can recollect yourself and reflect on what your purpose is to-day; you can resolve to lead a Christian life, and then by reciting an Our Father and a Hail Mary beseech the Lord for his assistance, invoking at the same time the assistance of the Holy Mother of God and the saints. You can do the same in the evening before retiring to rest; you can offer up to God an appropriate prayer of thanksgiving, ask pardon, and recommend yourself to God's merciful protection. Is it hard to do this? Can you make excuse that you have no time? Where is the man who has no time to spare to take the necessary food for his support? Now daily prayers are to our souls in a certain sense what food is to our body; without it the soul pines away and finally dies.

O Christian father, for your own sake and for the love you bear your children, make it an invariable rule to always say your morning and evening prayers. Must not a single glance at your children move you to this duty? They likewise need that grace and protection which is obtained by prayer.

A few years ago a celebrated Jesuit father gave a course of lectures to the men of the higher class of society in a certain city. In the concluding lecture, the subject of which was, what they should do in order to persevere and render fruitful the good acquired during the mission, he said: "One of the first and principal means is to assist at the daily sacrifice of the Mass." We do not know whether the advice of the pious father was followed or not; we however heartily approve of it.

Why do so few men assist at the daily sacrifice of the Mass? Is it less necessary for them than for women? We have shown above that it is more necessary for men, on account of the greater dangers to which they are exposed and the greater difficulties they encounter. Or are men so circumstanced that they cannot attend? Have they no time? Of course some have not. But how many would have time if they took the trouble to rise half an hour earlier? They could if they had a mind to. What a daily blessing that would be! How greatly would the holy sacrifice strengthen and fortify the Christian spirit! How abundantly would it draw down the blessings of heaven upon their daily actions; blessings in which the children may participate if the father, while assisting at Mass, remembers them and recommends them to the care and protection of Him who was the children's friend.

3. *"Remember that thou keep holy the Sabbath Day.*

We have advisedly quoted here God's own words. Is it not probable, that as he insists so positively on the sanctification of that day, that his "*Remember*" was in a special manner addressed to men—to fathers? Who stand more in need of sanctifying the Sunday? If, as has been said above, the avocations of the majority of men have a tendency to draw their minds away from spiritual things and lead them astray in various ways, of what importance is the Sunday, particularly for them? God enjoins rest from all worldly and servile work or occupation. Man thereby having leisure to enter into himself, to occupy his mind with the affairs of his higher calling, rekindles in himself the flames of holy desires, and thus divine grace increases in his heart and he becomes a new man.

But what if a man or father cares not to renew his spirit on this sacred day, if he does not refrain from servile work, if he occupies his mind with worldly cares and has little or no regard for God's word or for pious and devout exercises? Does it not reflect disgrace on his character as a Christian, and will not his soul be lost?

O Christian father, keep the Sunday holy according to God's will. Be convinced that to work out your salvation, it is necessary to be a good Christian;

that is, a good father to your children. Who can doubt that this is your sacred duty on account of the good example which you are obliged to give? It is necessary for the eternal welfare of your children that they learn and become early accustomed to keep the Sunday holy, according to the most holy will of God. Will they do this when they see how careless and indifferent their father is on this point? But we only mention this in passing. We are speaking here of the worthy observance of the Sunday, as it is a means, a most necessary means, for a father to preserve and strengthen within him a true Christian spirit. And indeed in the worthy observance of the Sunday alone you have an almost certain proof that he is a true Christian father, and as such will give his children a true Christian education. Let this then be your inviolable rule: All work, all worldly cares must cease on Sunday unless in case of necessity! "It is the day of the Lord, thou shalt do no work on it," says the Lord. To excite devotion and fervor, to strengthen yourself to work out your eternal salvation, is what you must aim at on Sunday. Therefore, as far as circumstances will permit, assist devoutly at the Holy Sacrifice of the Mass, hear the word of God, assist at the other sacred services of the Church, read pious books, etc. And then if you wish to recreate and amuse yourself you will not pass the bounds of moderation.

Happy that family whose father, and consequently all the other members, keep the Sunday holy in this manner. The spirit of Christian piety will flourish more and more, and the most precious gifts of heaven will be poured into its bosom.

It only remains now to treat of one more means to acquire and preserve a true Christian spirit, and this is the crown of all the rest.

4. *Arise and Eat.*

Thus the angel addressed the prophet Elias when he was fleeing from the wrath of Jezabel. He was fatigued by his journey in the desert, and "he sat under a juniper tree" and fell asleep. The angel touched him, and said to him: "Arise and eat; for thou hast yet a great way to go" (III. Kings xix. 7).

How often do you receive holy communion? If you observe those who approach the table of the Lord on Sundays and holy days you will find that, as a rule, the number of women far exceeds that of the men. You may perhaps see some men, but very few. We will not, however, be too severe. We will grant for a moment that it appears to be more natural for women than for men to receive frequently the Holy Sacrament; that on this point every one is inclined to be indulgent if they do not receive so frequently. But this "not so frequently" occurs too often, and it is to be regretted that the appearance of men at the altar rails is of so rare occurrence, for their absence is very apt to awaken grave fears, particularly if they are fathers.

What is the reason of all this? Can you find an explanation or an excuse for it in the position fathers occupy? Should we not expect them to receive holy communion more frequently? What is the reason?

Is it perhaps not necessary to receive holy communion frequently? We have seen that men, in order to lead a Christian life, have to overcome greater difficulties, that they meet with greater dangers, and that they have harder battles to fight than women. Men, therefore, need greater grace than women. And where will they find more strength, courage, and grace than in the worthy reception of the sacraments of penance and the Holy Eucharist? No one who understands the ways of the spiritual life can deny that one of the principal reasons why men possess so little sentiment and feeling for divine things, why they are so attached to the world and to sin, is that they seldom receive the holy sacraments. The spiritual life becomes weak because it receives only at long intervals that nourishment which our divine Saviour left for that purpose; and consequently the spiritual life dies out. "Unless you eat the flesh of the Son of man and drink his blood you shall not have life in you" (John, vi. 54).

The life of the body must be sustained and strengthened by daily food and nourishment; the life of the soul likewise needs food and strength, which is given by divine grace. Now this food, strength, and grace the Lord has prepared for us in a special manner in the sacrament of the Holy Eucharist; there the Christian must seek it. If he neglect it, the grace necessary to work out his salvation will be wanting. The Lord will withhold it from him because he does not use the means provided by him to obtain it.

O fathers! would that you all understood how **necessary** holy communion is to you in order to acquire and persevere in piety! How necessary for you to receive frequently this holy food, as it is the means to acquire that piety which is of such importance to you and so necessary for the good education of your children.*

And why not? Why do you so seldom receive holy communion? Is it impossible for you to receive it more frequently? Confess the truth; it all depends on your own will. He who

---

* It must be observed that a becoming zeal in receiving holy communion is all the more a duty of the father, on account of his obligation to give his children good example in this important matter. Will the children go to communion often if the father is negligent in this duty?

earnestly and sincerely wills it will find every few weeks the time necessary for confession and communion. But the fact is, the real reason why these holy sacraments are so seldom received lies in the want of love of God, in the want of zeal for your soul's salvation.

Here then you should resolve to keep this as a sacred rule: To frequently receive holy communion. This will cherish and foster the spirit of Christian piety within you. This will give you strength and power to overcome the difficulties you may meet with in the practice of virtue. This will, in a special manner, make you a good Christian father.

The Work of a Christian Father.

WE have dwelt at some length on this subject in the preceding chapters. We were then working at the foundation of a structure that reaches into eternity, and the foundation of such a structure must be solid and firm. The father must be Christian; all depends on this. All will admit that the welfare of the world, especially in our day, depends, after God, on the father and mother. But it is asked, What qualifications must a father and mother possess in order to promote this welfare? The answer is that although there are many qualifications required to attain this end, the first and most important is that a father and mother be truly Christian in spirit.

Now if we have succeeded in showing how important a Christian spirit is for a father in order to succeed in the education of his children it will be readily admitted that it was very proper to treat of this subject at some length. It was not enough to tell a father how important it is, and to encourage him; it was necessary also to explain in detail what is to be avoided and what is to be done in order to acquire this true Christian spirit and persevere in it.

We will now speak of the vocation of the father, of what a Christian father must do to execute faithfully that great work—the education of his children. It is not, however, our purpose to treat the subject of the Christian education of children in all its details; it would swell our little book to a large volume, which few would be able to purchase and read. We intend simply to explain the most necessary points of this subject. This will be enough. A true Christian spirit is, according to our supposition, the most necessary thing for a father. If he understands this well he will undoubtedly, with the divine assistance, be able to discover the right way in the education of his children.*

---

*I cannot forbear here to advise fathers to read our little book, THE CHRISTIAN MOTHER. What has been said in it is of equal importance to the Christian father. That natural *love* which he has for his children must be blessed and glorified by faith and grace ("Christian Mother," page 40) before he can succeed in the work of education. Let him also read of the *dowry* (page 54), in order that he may know that the nature and characteristics of the father influence the children for good or evil. He should also do his part, that that consecrated atmosphere or holy influence on which the results of a good education so necessarily depend, should pervade the household (page 63). If it is the mother's duty to lead the children to a knowledge of the Christian truths, it is no less the duty of the father (page 69). In like manner what is said of the *guard of holy innocence* (page 95); of *direction* (page 106), and lastly of the mother in prayer, is equally applicable and valuable to the father. As in this, our little work, we treat of

I. "Lay up to Yourself Treasures."

In speaking of the education of children the above sounds as if we meant to insinuate a doctrine which, according to Christian principles, ought not to hold the first place, namely, the worldly welfare of the children, or the acquiring of riches for them.

But let us explain. The labor and exertions of the father for the temporal welfare of his children is, of course, a part of his work, even according to Christian principles. The Lord has imposed on him the task of acquiring what is necessary or desirable for the proper support of his children, for their clothing, for their instruction in useful and necessary things, and also that he may be

---

still other questions in reference to a good Christian education. THE CHRISTIAN FATHER and THE CHRISTIAN MOTHER form, in some respects, but one work in two parts. We would wish, therefore, that the father read the latter, and the mother the former.

able to assist them, at the proper time, to earn their own livelihood according to their station in life. But it is not necessary to exhort or encourage fathers to do this for their children; they feel a natural impulse to do it. And indeed we have no fault to find with a father for exerting himself to provide comfortably for his children if he does not forget what is more important—his and their eternal welfare. It is right for father and mother to strive to leave a competency to their children, providing they at the same time secure for them that rich treasure, the grace of true Christian piety and the fear of God. But this worldly wealth would be too dearly bought, no matter how valuable it might be, if in order to obtain it parents and children should suffer spiritual damage. It would not be difficult to prove by examples taken from everyday life that those children to whom much has been given are not the happiest, or as happy as those who have received from their parents a good Christian education.

We therefore do not speak here of riches which are to be left to the children, but of riches which the father is to lay up for himself by working for the temporal welfare of his children.

Let us begin with a story. We knew a man who was not blessed with children. One day while listening to a sermon the following words made a strong impression on him: "Whosoever shall receive this child in my name receiveth me" (Luke ix. 48). These words left him no rest, and this thought troubled his mind: Perhaps God had not given him children that he might take care of poor, destitute orphan children. He resolved to obey the inspiration, and his wife seconded his resolution with all her heart. It was not long before he received the first child, an orphan. Others soon followed, until he had six in all—six poor, forsaken orphans. No one who did not know would ever have thought they were not his own with such energy did he follow his daily avocations in order to provide for his numerous little family. Everything necessary was provided for them, every care taken of them.

What impression, Christian father, does this story make on you? You who well know from experience what an amount of labor, sacrifice, patience, and care one—two—three—six children cost from day to day, for years! We are not mistaken when we say that this foster-father "had laid up to himself treasures in heaven" (Matth. vi. 20).

We must admit this to be the case if we consider how much these children daily cost him and how much he had to exert himself to provide for them. If we remember that the Lord will not permit a cup of cold water given for His sake to go unrewarded, how great

The Work of a Christian Father.

must be the reward of this father who for years had daily given and done so much.

Well, then, let us make the application. Do you, O father, do less for your own children than this noble-minded foster-father did for his adopted children? O no; you do the same, or, perhaps, even more. What expense you must go to daily—and for years! How you must work and exert yourself day after day and year after year! How much you must suffer and endure all this time! Can we not say of you what we have said of that foster-father: What a great treasure you have laid up to yourself in heaven, and what a reward awaits you! Or does it make any difference that you work and suffer for your own children while he worked and suffered for those whom he had adopted? Are not your children equally as pleasing to God as the adopted children? Or is it less meritorious to labor and suffer for your own children? No, it is the same.

But let us proceed. What is it that renders the action of the foster-father so meritorious? Is it not because he worked and suffered for those poor orphans? Of course it is; and yet there is still a better reason for it. *It is because he did it for the love of God and out of Christian love for the children.* Here we have at last come to the point. Do you, O Christian father, do all you do for your children for the love of God and out of true Christian love for your children? Then you are like that foster-father, and we can likewise say of you: What a treasure of merit, what a reward you will reap!

In this way the whole life of a father is an uninterrupted work of mercy. And what a work of mercy! What else is it than relieving the wants of our neighbor for God's sake and out of Christian love? Now almost the whole life of a Christian father consists in working, caring, and exerting himself for his children—to give them food, to clothe and lodge them, to teach, counsel, and console them, to pardon them, and, if sick, to heal them. If a father is animated by love for God and for his children his life will be a succession of works of charity and mercy.

How highly does God value works of mercy! How great the reward promised for time and eternity!

Behold then, O Christian father, you are in a position to reap these blessings of Christian mercy during your life and for all eternity. It is only necessary that all you do out of natural love for your children be not done from necessity, but from love of God and Christian love for them.

You should consider your children as confided to you by God, who is your Master; and what you do and suffer for them you should consider as belonging to your vocation, and thus accept and bear all with a cheerful heart, from love to God and your children. Then indeed will your daily life be pleasing to God and a work of mercy to your children. Works of mercy thus interwoven in a man's life are a perpetual prayer to God for grace and mercy for him who has performed them. Behold how rich you can become by means of your children! The more there are and the more you suffer and endure for them the richer you will be.

Will not this reflection reconcile you to the hardships of which your children are the cause, and preserve you from ill-humor and impatience? Human efforts and exertions never find so rich a reward as when they are performed in the service of him who is the great rewarder, or when they are done for the good of those who are so dear to him. In fact, the most profitable work on earth is the Christian work of a father—of parents for their children.

How much then it is to be regretted that parents—that fathers—see nothing in their daily labor for their children but the unpleasantness and burden of it, and who therefore perform such labor as if under compulsion and against their will! They thus make that work an almost unbearable cross; they lose the great reward promised them; they even commit sin! How much it is to be regretted that parents are but too often actuated only by natural motives in their efforts for their children, and therefore that they will receive no reward in eternity.

Take care, therefore, Christian father, to labor for your children in a Christian spirit. This you can do if you are truly a Christian father.

II. Government.—Discipline.

It is clear from the above words that we intend to speak of education, and to explain a point which is undoubtedly of great importance to a father in bringing up his children. According to the words of the divine Father, "Man is the head of the woman" (I. Cor. xi. 3), and consequently the head of the whole family. He is therefore the master of the house, and must rule and govern, of course in a Christian spirit, because he is a Christian father, and as such must show love and affection for those who are and must be subject to him. "Husbands, love your wives as Christ also loved the Church" (Eph. v. 25). And is there a Christian father, who does not love his children? His government must therefore be regulated by love and moderation, without, however, ceasing to be a government. He must guide and direct if the work of education is to advance.

Where is there a State that has no head or supreme magistrate? We all know that without such a head no State or society can exist. There will and must be an emperor, king, president, congress, or some other supreme authority. This authority enforces existing laws and sanctions laws which are to be enacted. It watches and sees that the laws are observed, and it punishes the transgressors of the law. You will find the same order of things existing in the Church. There is a head over all, and heads over communities; there is law and supervision of its observance; there is punishment inflicted on the transgressors of the law. It cannot be otherwise; it must be so, in State and Church, if society is to exist and prosper.

Now the same is the case in the family. If the family is to prosper, if the education of the children is to advance, **there must** be a governing hand ruling all things; the family must have a head, and God has in fact appointed a head for it—it is the father. He (with the mother) lays down the law, the rules, the order to be observed; he watches over the discipline of the family and exercises the right of punishment.

(1.) LAW, RULE, AND ORDER.

The family, according to the providence of God, is the nursery for Church and State. In it the children should grow up to be useful citizens and good Christians, so that on leaving the paternal roof they may be worthy members of Church and State.

There are such nurseries established by the Church, called seminaries, where young men are taught to become worthy members of the ministry. To fit the pupils to become good priests by instilling into them the true spirit of their vocation, and thus render them capable of performing the duties of their high calling; such is the object in establishing seminaries.

Everything in a seminary is directed to this end. There are rules for the daily life and conduct of the students, compiled by the superiors after long experience and mature deliberation, the details of which are calculated to regulate the life and occupations of the students in such a manner as to attain the end and purpose of such an institution. The hour of rising in the morning and retiring at night is fixed by rule; there is a fixed time for breakfast, dinner, and supper, and for the daily recreations. Certain spiritual exercises are prescribed, such as morning and evening prayer, meditation, hearing Mass, receiving the sacraments, etc. There is also a time fixed for study. Rules are laid down to regulate the intercourse of the students with each other, etc. This is the rule, the law, and the superior of the seminary regulates all accordingly. He has an eye to the observance of the rules; he admonishes, and, if need be, punishes the transgressors. The more faithfully he does this the better he understands how to lead the students to observe conscientiously and strictly the rules and laws, and to regulate their daily life according to them; and thus the object and aim of the seminary is attained, and the students will go forth worthy and zealous priests. Without rule, law, and order, and the observance of them, this could not be the case.

We have called the family the nursery for Church and State. If, then, it is to fulfil its purpose, and bring up useful and worthy members of Church and State, it must, like a seminary, have its laws, rules, and regulations, and the father, who is the superior and head of the family, must see that these rules and laws are duly observed.

¶. We do not require for the family the rules and laws of the seminary, which determine and regulate the minutest details of daily life; it would be impossible to observe such rules in the family. Yet there must be certain rules and laws in the family if the education of the children is to be successfully conducted. Without them nothing will succeed; without them the children will neither be good members of society nor good Christians.

There is a general rule and law for every Christian family; it is the law of the divine will. This is an indispensable law, and the father must see that it is observed. Nothing can be tolerated that is contrary to the divine will, and what God commands must be done.

According to this, all improper customs and habits are to be excluded from the Christian family—the habit of giving way to anger, of scolding and swearing; the bad habit of lying and backbiting; in a special manner all dissolute and impious conversation; every disedifying remark against the doctrines and customs of the Church,—all these must be absolutely forbidden.

On the contrary, all that is truly Christian and in accordance with God's will ought to be cherished in the Christian household. Grace is said before and after meals; prayer is said morning and evening; servile work is not permitted on Sunday or holy days, unless through necessity; the members of the household attend Mass and assist at the other devotions of the Church; they go to confession, and receive holy communion; they observe the days of fasting and abstinence, etc.; the works of charity and mercy are not forgotten, for love and sympathy animate all; and to complete the list we must include sobriety, purity, diligence, fervor, cleanliness, etc.

Need we add that it is a great blessing for children when such laws and order exist in the family, and when they grow up under their influence and become accustomed to them. Will they not become good men and women and good Christians? But poor and unfortunate children when there is no such order in the family; when they are constantly witnessing transgressions against the divine will, and offences against Christian propriety and morals! Will it not require a miracle to make such children good under the circumstances?

We have thus far explained the principal point of our subject, for the proper method of bringing up children consists in this, that law and order should reign in the family, and that the father and mother should enforce them. We however wish to treat of this subject more at length.

As the father has been appointed by God the head of the family he has in virtue of that appointment the authority to make laws and rules for the members of the family, particularly for his children; and if his rules and laws are not contrary to the will of God they have the same binding force as the commandments of God. In virtue of this authority, then, the father should ordain and determine all that is necessary and useful to bring up his children good citizens and Christians. For that purpose he might select some rules from the ecclesiastical seminary, and he can insist on their observance. The hour of rising in the morning and retiring in the evening; the time for breakfast, dinner, and supper, and the time for work and recreation; all these should be fixed and determined, and faithfully observed as far as possible.

We say as far as possible, for we know very well that through necessity exceptions must be made; but we know also that it is very possible to keep the exceptions in the minority, and thus on the whole the rule remains in force. This is of great importance for the children, for you cannot sufficiently appreciate the blessing and the advantage of accustoming children to a well regulated life. It causes a certain freshness and joy of heart in daily life which renders easy the performance of their daily duties. "God," says St. Augustine, "is a God of order; he, therefore, who lives according to order lives according to God." And St. Bernard says, "My brethren, I warn you in the Lord, be diligent in preserving order that order may preserve you."

It is not to be left to the pleasure of the children when they may leave the house or when they should return.

The father or mother must give them permission to go and appoint the time when they must return. An hour should be set when all the members of the family must be at home, or the doors closed and locked on them.

As it is the duty of the father and mother to assign to each member of the family that part of the daily work which each must perform, they should have regard to the ability of their little subjects, to their likes and dislikes for certain kinds of work, and, if possible, gratify their inclination; they should, moreover, once and for all, give a certain work to a certain member of the family; the work is thereby made easier, the workman acquires a certain independence, and all is done well. Let us add to this that the father and mother must determine when the sacraments are to be received; they must also establish fixed rules in regard to going out to evening parties, inviting company, etc.; and finally, it must be understood that sons and daughters cannot do what they please, particularly if it be of importance, without the knowledge and consent of the father.

We have now given a sketch of the rules and laws of a Christian family. They must apply to all the members of the household, and the duty of the father is to

(2) SEE THAT THEY ARE OBSERVED.

If we return once more to the seminary we will find that according as the superior has at heart the education of good ecclesiastics he will not only recognize the necessity and importance of certain rules to attain the desired end, but he will also enforce a faithful observance of them. And in like manner every good, intelligent father who has the welfare of his children at heart will be very careful that the rules and regulations which he has made are carefully and strictly observed by them. This is the father's will; the child knows it, and therefore it is its duty to govern itself accordingly. The child must be obedient. Of course we presuppose that the father does not order or command anything contrary to the will of God.

Obedience. In the faithful exercise of this virtue is the greatest blessing for a child. By it that self-will which is such a hindrance to the fulfilment of God's will and to a true Christian life is broken. If a child be accustomed to subject its will to that of its father it will be so much easier for it to obey the laws of superiors, of the civil authority, of God. If obedience to the laws of the State makes a good citizen, if obedience to the precepts of the Church makes a good Christian, then a father fulfils in a special manner the requirements of his vocation when he demands strict obedience to his will and accustoms the child to obey. It will thus grow up a good citizen and a good Christian.

This ought to be at all times dear to the father's heart. His will must be the guide of the child, and it must understand that whatsoever the father orders or commands—of course with due reflection—must be done. Nothing will induce a good, intelligent father to change his mind simply for the whim of his child, not even when he is compelled to have recourse to stern measures to enforce obedience. This may be the reason why man's will is more resolute, determined, and stronger than that of woman, that the father may remain firm in demanding an unconditional obedience from his children, when the mother, on account of her more tender feeling, might give way to their importunities, wishes, and prayers. The father can prevent this, and the child will be spared the consequences which such unseasonable giving way might cause.

You will frequently hear parents complain that their children, particularly the grown-up ones, will not obey. We admit that a certain perverseness may be the cause of this deplorable conduct of grown-up sons and daughters; we assert, nevertheless, that the parents, and particularly the father, in not enforcing obedience at the proper time, was the cause of this misconduct. Indeed we need not be astonished at the disobedience of sons and daughters when the parents are so indulgent to them in their childhood, permitting them to follow their own will, to be stubborn and obstinate, and to have their own way in everything. This, then, is in most cases the cause of the disgraceful conduct which so grieves and mortifies the parents and causes so much annoyance. This alone should suffice to show that children should be taught to obey and made to obey. Fathers who accustom their children to obey from their childhood work for their own benefit as well as for the welfare of their children, who will in time be a source of joy and consolation to them.

Thus great and abundant blessings follow obedience, because the road to true happiness is to be found in doing the father's will. According to the opinion of intelligent persons no greater benefit can be granted a child than to teach it perfect obedience. When advice and admonition fail to make the child obedient the father does not hesitate, but considers it his duty to exercise his

(3) RIGHT TO PUNISH.

to enforce obedience. St. Paul says: "For what son is there whom the father does not correct?" (Heb. xii. 7), and he adds, "Persevere, therefore, under discipline. God dealeth with you as with his sons" meaning that when he punishes you he shows himself a father. "Whom the Lord loveth he chastiseth, and he scourgeth every son whom he receiveth" (Heb. xii. 6); that is, whom he graciously intends to lead to goodness and eternal life. There appears to be a contradiction in these words "whom the Lord loveth he chastiseth," and yet such is not the case, for they contain a salutary truth. The Apostle explains it in the eleventh verse, where he says: "All chastisement for the present indeed seemeth not to bring with it joy, but sorrow: but afterwards it will yield to them that are exercised by it"—exercised by chastisement unto Christian perfection, "the most peaceful fruit of justice." The sufferings with which God visits his children to preserve them from sin and to lead them to Christian perfection are nothing when compared to the sufferings caused by sin. If, then, punishment or chastisement is a means to obtain happiness it is an evidence of God's love for us when he inflicts it.

In this our heavenly Father is the model for human fathers. The laws of God, the precepts of the Church, and the rules laid down by the father are the way in which the child must walk to become a useful citizen and a good Christian, and gain temporal and eternal happiness. That, therefore, which tends to keep the child in this road, or lead it back to it when astray, is beneficial to it, and its application is a sign of genuine love for the child.

When, therefore, a child is led by bad inclinations, bad example, or by temptations of the enemy to depart from the right way, and when it will not be induced to return by mildness, advice, and admonition, the father will adopt sterner means; he will punish and chastise his child to curb its perverse will and overcome its obstinacy.

This "for the present indeed seemeth not to bring with it joy" neither for father nor child. The little one sighs, weeps, and pleads. The father's natural feelings revolt; his heart is moved by the pitiful appeals of the child. And yet he must overcome all this. He must wield the rod, and if he fail to do this his injudicious forbearance will foster disobedience with all its evil consequences, and cause the child miseries in comparison with which the transient sufferings from deserved punishment will appear as nothing. On the other hand, punishment inflicted in the proper manner and at the proper time will regulate the will of the child, subdue its stubborn haughtiness, and conquer its perversity. Such punishment will lead the child into the way of God's holy will and obtain for it "the peaceful fruit of justice."

According to this it appears to be a sacred duty of fathers to punish their children when occasion requires it. As evidence of this paternal obligation we may refer to the terrible punishment which the Lord inflicted on the high-priest Heli because he did not correct and punish his two sons, who, priests like himself, performed their duty negligently and gave great scandal to the people. "In that day," said the Lord, "I will raise up against Heli all the things I have spoken concerning his house, for I have foretold unto him that I will judge his house forever, for iniquity, because he knew that his sons did wickedly, and did not chastise them" (I. Kings iii. 12, 13). "I will begin and I will make an end." And soon after these words were fulfilled. In a battle against the Philistines he permitted "Israel to be overthrown... and there was an exceeding great slaughter, for there fell of Israel thirty thousand footmen. And the ark of God was taken; and the two sons of

Heli, Ophni and Phinees, were slain" (I. Kings iv. 10, 11). And as a messenger gave an account of it to Heli, who was ninety-eight years old, "he fell from his stool backwards by the door, and broke his neck, and died" (verse 18). Can we still doubt that it is a strict obligation for fathers to chastise their children as the occasion may require, and when necessity demands?

We say advisedly, *as the occasion may require.* The reason why children are punished is to make them obedient, or to bring them back to obedience. If this end can be gained by mild means, such as teaching, advising, and admonishing, it would be an abuse of authority to inflict corporal punishment. How often do children fail more through ignorance and want of thought than through malice or perverse will? Now if you teach them, and warn them to be more careful in future, you will almost always gain your point; but if in such cases you inflict corporal punishment when not deserved it acts injuriously on the mind of the child, particularly if it be naturally timid. In every case where a child can be brought to a sense of its duty by kind though earnest words and fatherly advice this method of correction should be preferred to corporal punishment.

We have said where necessity demands it and when it is useful. It is the interest which the father has in the welfare of his child that causes him to punish it, that it may correct its faults and lead a good life. The great Father of mankind had this object in view when he gave man authority to inflict punishment. To be carried away by impatience and anger at the misconduct and failings of your children, or to be led by momentary aversion, ill-will, or bad humor to inflict punishment on them, is to abuse the authority which God has reposed in you. Such punishment is a mere gratification of your own passion, and thus while you correct your child's fault you commit a greater one yourself. It is evident that such treatment is worse than useless. And how can it be otherwise when it proceeds from such improper motives and is inflicted so injudiciously.

But let us suppose that the punishment inflicted is in keeping with the nature of the child and its offence, yet in the supposition made above the father will scarcely be able to inflict it with the necessary calmness. The punishment will be accompanied with abuse, reproaches, anger, and too great severity or cruelty. When even a deserved punishment is thus inflicted, the child is outraged by its father and its feelings are wounded. It feels the injustice of the punishment inflicted in this way, and is shocked at seeing its own father rising as an enemy and treating it with such cruelty, and in such an unworthy and passionate manner. A deadly blow is thus given to its young heart, and the veneration which it naturally had for its father is replaced by a sentiment of contempt and scorn!

This is certainly a punishment that will not only not cure the child's faults and failings, but will increase them.

Alas, how often are such methods adopted by fathers in punishing their children! What a responsibility! Those appointed by God to be the father and friend of their children become their worst enemies! The manner in which they inflict punishment does their children incalculable injury. St. Paul had this in view when in writing to the Ephesians he said: "And you, fathers, provoke not your children to anger, but bring them up in the discipline and correction of the Lord" (Eph. vi. 4). The Apostle means to say, keep your children under discipline, punish them when necessary, but as God does, who punishes with justice, mercy, and indulgence. Writing to the Colossians the same Apostle says: "Fathers, provoke not" by unreasonable punishment "your children to indignation, lest they be discouraged" (Coloss. iii. 21).

Thus far we have spoken of the manner in which punishment is inflicted, but how often do not parents commit another fault by want of care and intelligence in the selection and choice of the proper punishment to be inflicted.

The child must be punished, but there are many kinds of punishments. If we judged by the conduct of some parents we would conclude that there is but one kind—flogging. The children are flogged with rods and sticks and beaten with clubs; their ears are cuffed and wrenched, their hair pulled and the first thing that comes to hand is hurled at their heads.

Now we think, and with good reason, that some of these punishments are entirely unworthy of a Christian father (and mother), particularly when inflicted in a fit of anger. Common-sense and Christian forbearance forbid a parent to punish his child in this way.

There are, however, some punishments which are permitted; for instance, a father may use a rod or whip, and according to circumstances he may box the ears or slap the cheek, for there are some children who cannot be brought to a sense of their duty by any other means. There are cases also where punishment should be inflicted on the spot—then and there.

But to insist on punishing indiscriminately all children, and in every case by corporal punishment, is most unreasonable. As we have seen, it deprives the children of the beneficial effects of the chastisement. We have said above that there are different kinds of punishments. It is punishment for a child to deprive it of certain things that it loves—if it is not permitted to play at a certain time; if it is kept waiting a short time for its dinner or supper; if forbidden to make visits, and to play at times with its little companions; if deprived of its toys, etc. It is also a punishment to oblige the child to do something that is unpleasant or disagreeable; for instance, to remain alone for a short time; to do some work for which it feels a repugnance; to wear for a time old and shabby clothes; to do something that is humiliating, etc.

Among such a variety the parents can always find that which is best adapted to attain the end for which the punishment is inflicted—the amendment of the child. Who can deny that mild punishments do more good to a naturally timid child than harsh and severe treatment does? Punishments that are proper for small children are not adapted to grown up boys and girls. Some humiliating task should be given for faults that originate in pride and self-esteem, and sensuality should be met by privation of what is gratifying to the senses.

Can you find a sensible artisan or mechanic who, having all the various tools necessary for his work, will take the first tool that comes to hand, whether it be the right one or not? You certainly cannot. The artisan will select that tool best fitted for the work he is at; he won't take a saw to plane a board or a hammer to saw it. Now the education (bringing up) of children is a most important work; and yet when parents who are engaged in this work have to inflict punishment they apply the first that suggests itself instead of selecting carefully the best and most useful method!

The counsel and advice which we have given to fathers are certainly not very easy to carry out. It is indeed easier not to punish at all than to punish in the proper manner. To exercise the right of inflicting punishment requires great devotion to the welfare of the child; it requires great pains, much reflection and deliberation, and not a little self-sacrifice. But it is a sacred duty and a condition of the father's eternal welfare. And here are verified the words of the Lord: "The kingdom of heaven suffereth violence; and the violent bear it away" (Matth. xi. 12). Besides, if the right of punishing is properly and faithfully exercised it will bear precious fruit in the children, and is therefore well worthy all the father's sacrifices and pains. The father who does his duty in this regard will reap a great reward here on earth and still a greater reward in eternity for his cares, anxieties, and sacrifices; while those who do not keep their children under discipline, or do not do so in a proper manner, suffer grief, affliction, anxiety, and trouble in this world from the perverse conduct of their children. And what will be their lot in eternity!

III. Paternal Cares.

Let us imagine a father who strives to follow the advice and counsel given above. His children are safe as long as they are under his care and guidance. But children do not always remain in the secure enclosure of their father's house. They have much intercourse with those outside, and a time will come when sons and daughters must leave the paternal roof. From this new duties arise. Let us mention them.

(1) SUPERINTENDENCE OF CHILDREN.

The father (and mother) cannot possibly have their children, old and young, constantly under their immediate surveillance. Work and various occupations will separate them for a longer or shorter time from the children; and the latter are not always at home, they are at some employment, at school, or at play, etc.

On such occasions the children may be in great danger. They meet with other children or adults whose conversation scandalize them; they have intercourse with persons who may even endeavor to lead them into sin; they go to places where their faith and their innocence are in great danger; they attend pleasure parties and maintain friendships of a dangerous character.

Children are inexperienced; if not warned in time they rush into the greatest dangers and are ruined! They are inconsiderate; they are easily carried away by their impulses, which lead them to destruction. They are dependent on others and are with little difficulty led astray.

Will not a father who knows and reflects on these things take care of his child, and as far as lies in his power protect it from the threatened danger? Is this not his most sacred duty?

We admit that under certain circumstances the situation of the child cannot be made perfectly safe and secure, do what you may. But you must do what you can. And indeed much can be done in this particular if you have a good will and do not shirk trouble and sacrifice. The example of really good parents is a proof of this. It cannot of course be accomplished without care and perseverance. But there are some fathers who are not willing to trouble themselves much about it, and who, therefore, leave their children without any supervision and permit them to do about as they please. How many children are perverted and lost because fathers (and mothers) are wanting in watchfulness and care!

It has often been remarked that many fathers take more care of their cattle than of their children. They are very careful to preserve their dumb brutes from danger or injury, while they carelessly permit their children to be exposed to even greater dangers. How true and just is not this comparison in many cases! It will, at the proper time, rise up in judgment against such fathers and establish the justice of their eternal damnation.

It is therefore the most sacred duty of a Christian father to do all he can in this regard. First of all, the father (and mother) should endeavor to learn where the son or daughter goes, particularly if they are to be away from home for a considerable time; they should also try to know with what company they associate.

Moreover, it is important for the father to know the character of the places they frequent as well as that of the persons they meet there; to know what goes on at such places, what amusements are indulged in, etc. If the father sincerely wills it he can find ways and means to acquire such knowledge. He will, according to circumstances, call the son or daughter to give an account of themselves during their absence from home; he will investigate the matter, and with prudence and care he may draw the necessary information from others, or perhaps his own experience will enable him to form a correct judgment of such visits and amusements, and how dangerous the familiar intercourse between young people of both sexes may be.

Possessed of this knowledge, the father will govern himself accordingly. First of all, when his children are about to leave the house he must know where they are going. If they have been accustomed to this rule in their younger years they will the more readily observe it as they grow up.

What after mature deliberation he considers dangerous to the child, in view of its age and its qualities of mind and body, he will strictly forbid; for instance, association with certain children, visits to certain houses, or, in the case of older children, the company of certain persons, the indulgence in certain amusements, etc. The father will insist on the strict observance of his orders.

If he finds that a son or daughter has disobeyed his orders in these matters he will earnestly warn and advise him or her, in case the disobedience was more the result of ignorance or want of reflection than of malice; but if in spite of his repeated advice and warnings his orders have been wilfully disobeyed he will not fail to inflict condign punishment. Earnestness, firmness, and resolution are required, and in certain circumstances even great severity may be necessary, particularly where there is evident danger of sin if the forbidden practices are not promptly discontinued.

It will be a great help to a father in attaining his object if order, regularity, and rule reign in his household, and if his children have accustomed themselves to this order and regularity, particularly the order requiring them to be home at a fixed hour. At any rate, if permission is given to be absent from home the time of their return must be determined, and no excuse should be admitted in case of failure.

There are cases where there is danger in attending certain parties, etc., and yet the father cannot well refuse permission to his son or daughter to attend; in such cases he should accompany them himself, or appoint a responsible person to see to them.

These are only a few hints given in a matter in which the individual cases differ so widely from each other that it is impossible to give a rule for each particular case. But what has been said will enable the father to deal with such cases as circumstances may require.

Would to God that all fathers and mothers would do their duty in this matter. How many sins would be prevented and how many children saved from ruin. How many have committed the most deplorable errors, by which the happiness of their lives have been destroyed and their immortal souls lost, all on account of parents neglecting to watch carefully over their children. Woe to the parents of such unfortunate children.

Arise then, Christian fathers, ponder and reflect on the duties of your vocation. Be watchful, and take care of those children whom God has entrusted to thee.*

---

*We take occasion here to call attention to a point which experience has taught us frequently becomes the occasion of great evils and sins to

(2) Son and Daughter Abroad.

The son and daughter leave their home in order to learn what is necessary for their future life, or to earn their own livelihood. The son as pupil in some institution, or as apprentice in

---

children—particularly to boys. It is, that they are allowed to have and to spend money in a way that is very dangerous and hurtful to them. This arises from undue kindness or indulgence of the father or mother in giving them money, or through neglect to keep it properly secured, so that the children can easily obtain it by stealth. Experience teaches that this indulgence or neglect on the part of parents, causes sad degeneracy in the children; leading to drink, to excesses, and even to dishonesty and theft. It makes our heart bleed to make such a discovery, and one is impelled to cry out: Oh, if the astonished father and mother could only be made to understand that they should withhold money from their children entirely, or give it only when necessary; that they should take the necessary precautions that the children cannot have access to the place where money is kept. Opportunity makes the thief.

a store or workshop, or as a servant. The daughter leaves the home of her childhood in order to acquire further accomplishments, or to earn her living as servant in another family.

Now a father who has above all the eternal welfare of his child at heart cannot see, without anxiety, his son or daughter go away where they will be no longer under his guardianship, protection, and influence. His soul is filled with anxiety when he reflects that his son or daughter may suffer from the fatal influence of bad example which persons of unchristian and immoral lives may give them; his mind is troubled at the thought of the evil effects the bad conversations and conduct of such persons may have on their young minds, as they are liable to undermine all the good principles of faith and morality which his children have received; he fears the enticements, inducements, and seductions of a wicked world with which his children must now come in contact.

And indeed he has cause to fear and tremble. Alas, how many young men and women who did so well under home influences have, after leaving the paternal roof good and virtuous children, suffered from the pernicious influence of their new homes; have lost by degrees those pious and religious sentiments with which they were imbued and given themselves up to sin and vice; have lost their innocence, their faith, and return to their home robbed of the most precious treasures of their lives!

Can, then, a Christian father (and mother) remain indifferent when they are compelled to let their children go abroad? Can they be indifferent to their fate? Impossible. They will rather, as is their duty, do their utmost to protect them from the threatened danger; they will endeavor as far as possible to preserve that faith and piety which was instilled into their hearts at home.

How strange! If you confide to the care of others anything that is precious and dear to you, you take every precaution that it will be returned in as good condition as when it left you; for example, if you loan money on interest you examine whether the party borrowing it can give sufficient security; you will not loan it if you see any danger of losing it. Now children, the most precious of all things, are placed out without any security that their eternal welfare is not at stake, or even when the contrary is known to be the fact. How inconsistent! What a responsibility!

It is true that in many cases it is sometimes almost impossible to do anything to protect the child, for it is not always possible to procure a situation for your child where you can find all as you would wish in regard to faith and morals. And yet the son and daughter must leave their homes; it cannot be helped.

It must, however, be admitted that there is in most cases on the part of the father an inconceivable indifference and unconcern which is inconsistent with a true Christian spirit. He has generally temporal prospects in view, and these alone he values and esteems. His son or daughter can learn in such a place much that is useful in a temporal point of view; in such a position they can acquire riches; in such a situation there are good prospects for the future, etc., etc. These considerations are enough to determine his mind. He does not ask if the son or daughter will be exposed to the danger of losing their faith or innocence of heart. This does not concern him; he even banishes the thought from his mind.

And what is the consequence? Of course the son and daughter may, in the circumstances into which they have been so recklessly thrown, become smart, intelligent, and learned; they may receive large salaries; fine prospects await them in the immediate future. But you will also find that with all these acquirements, hopes, and prospects they have lost that Christian feeling and sentiment which they had before; the exercise of the Christian virtues is not so familiar to them as formerly; they are slaves to wicked passions; they have lost purity of heart and suffered shipwreck of God's most precious gift—the faith. Will they be happy with all their other acquirements? Alas, not even here on earth will they be happy. No matter how frequently it has been denied, it is and will forever remain true that all earthly happiness, however great, will speedily vanish and leave the human heart empty and void unless it is built on the foundation of true Christian piety. And then eternity! Is the number of those unfortunates small who attribute their eternal damnation to those situations of earthly honors and riches in which they were so cruelly placed by their parents in their younger years?

But enough. There can be no doubt that the obligations of the father (and mother) do not cease when the children have left their home and the father cannot supervise their conduct. As long as the children have not arrived at that maturity of age and judgment which will enable them to take proper care of themselves the father must take care of them. If he cannot secure to all of them the advantages he desires he must at least do what he can. Experience teaches that good and conscientious parents can do much for their children by procuring proper situations for them. Such parents have their children's welfare at heart; they take great interest in this matter; they take pains to inquire and investigate, and spare no sacrifice. Nothing appears too difficult to such parents, because they really love their children and value their eternal welfare above all earthly things. Besides, the love they bear their children makes them inventive. And as they in this important matter have recourse to God by prayer, God enlightens their minds to a knowledge of the true course to follow, or turns circumstances to their advantage.

This is the manner in which truly pious Christian parents act. And if sometimes, even by their best efforts, they cannot obtain what they desire, and must be content with little or nothing, they will never place their children in situations where there is evident and certain danger to their faith and virtue, no matter how great the temporal advantages may be.

And when a child has left home the true Christian father (with the mother) will always have an eye on it, and as far as possible make inquiries about its conduct, etc. And should his previous hopes prove false, and he find that his son or daughter is in danger, he will not be careless and indifferent, but if matters cannot be remedied otherwise he will remove his child as soon as possible from such a place, and thus save its faith and virtue.

Here again the father cannot always do what his heart desires, nor can he do it as soon as he wishes; he does, however, what is possible. This he must do because it is the sacred duty of his vocation. What does a man do who has loaned money and fears that it may be lost? He takes measures to secure it. Now when it is a question of children, who are more precious and valuable than money, will a father not act in the same manner, and take measures to secure their temporal and eternal welfare?

Unfortunately this is done but too seldom; parents are in this particular too careless and indifferent, but when too late they must suffer the consequences. Their children will be their punishment. What grief and sorrow will such children cause their parents! Therefore "take care of them over whom you have been placed."

(3) Choice of a State of Life.

We intend to speak here of sons. Excepting in a few cases of a vocation to the religious state the future life of daughters is generally determined by circumstances of which we will treat further on. We speak now of the sons.

Well, what will our son become? Shall he study? Shall he learn a trade or an art? and which? Shall he be a soldier? or shall he devote his whole life to some ordinary occupation at home, or as a servant away from home? These are questions which very naturally arise in the mind of every father who has his son's welfare at heart.

There is unquestionably for every son, as for every child, a state of life which is most suitable to him, which is the best for him and most conducive to his welfare, considering his corporal and mental qualities, the circumstances in which he is placed, and the means he possesses. This state of life then is that which is most in harmony with God's will. It is his vocation.

From what we have thus far said it is evident that it is a matter of great importance for a son to know his vocation, to choose it, to prepare himself for it, and to follow it at the proper time. A vocation is a call to a certain state of life which is most in accord with the will of God, who rules from one end of the earth to the other and orders everything for the best. On this account has God bestowed upon your son the necessary gifts and ability, given him an inclination for his particular work, and placed him in circumstances where he can learn what is necessary for his state in life. If then we may hope that the young man will at the proper time enter on the duties of his vocation this hope will be increased by the well-founded expectation that the Lord will assist him with his divine grace in the vocation he has pointed out to him, and will in a special manner so regulate and order circumstances that he may perform the duties of his state of life and find eternal life.

If all this is calculated to impress us with the importance of a vocation it will appear still more forcible if we reflect that the vocation of a person to a certain state of life is the surest, the only way, to acquire true happiness and contentedness as far as it can be enjoyed here on earth, and that it is the best and surest way to eternal happiness. They who have missed their vocation are generally unhappy in their state of life, and as they find no pleasure in it and have no love for its obligations, they are very careless and negligent in the observance of them; thus they aggravate their own conscience, and become unhappy in themselves and obstacles to the welfare of others. A mistake in the choice of a vocation is, then, very dangerous, as it may finally lead to eternal ruin.

It is therefore of the greatest importance to a man to know and choose his vocation. And as the choice, in most cases, is made at an early age, when one does not possess mature judgment or experience to determine for one's self, the father (and mother) should assist their son by counsel and advice. For this purpose God in his wise providence confided children and youth to the care and guardianship of parents, that they might supply that which is wanting in them.

As we teach children that it is their sacred duty to consult their parents, and ask their advice before choosing a vocation, it is necessary that the father should study to know the vocation of his son in order to be able to give good advice.

This is sometimes not very difficult; the vocation of the son manifests itself in various ways. He shows very early a decided inclination for a particular trade, occupation, etc. This is a good sign that he has a vocation for it, especially if he possesses a natural aptitude for it and if there is no objection to it from other causes. Again, the vocation is known from circumstances; for example, the son is called to continue or carry on his father's business, or to follow his trade or occupation, always provided that he has no decided aversion to such occupation and is not wanting in the necessary qualifications for it.

However, the vocation of a son does not always show itself so clearly; you do not observe that natural inclination for a particular state in life, or if you do there are perhaps insurmountable obstacles in the way of such a choice; nor do circumstances throw any light on the subject. You must therefore reflect and take counsel in order to find the true vocation of your son.

Many errors are committed in this particular, and therefore there are so many mistaken vocations, with all their evil consequences.

The parents make a serious mistake when in selecting a vocation for their son they consult only selfish motives, inordinate desire of worldly gain, honors, etc. One father will select a calling for his son because it is more honorable, another because it is more profitable to himself. Thus many a son has to work either at home or in a shop or manufactory, and is prevented from learning the trade or business he desires. No regard is had for his inclination or abilities, or even for his eternal welfare.

This last reflection leads us to notice another very grievous mistake which parents make in choosing a state of life for their sons. Parents are almost always led to a choice by purely temporal motives, without considering the eternal welfare of their children. They make the choice and in a way force their choice on the son, while experience and his personal peculiarities show there is the greatest danger, and that such a state of life will prove an obstacle to his eternal happiness. This way of acting could be excused if there was a necessity for such a choice, but not even then when evident danger exists.

The main thing a father should have in view in choosing a state of life for his son is his eternal salvation. You must therefore in making your choice prefer that state which affords him the greatest protection against dangers to his soul. Is not the life of man, considered in the light of faith, a preparation for eternity? Is not man himself, as well as all he possesses, from God? And is not everything he possesses to be used to fit him for a happy eternity? As this happy eternity is the principal object of life it is also the principal object of every state of life, and therefore it is necessary in the choice of a state of life to examine and consider whether the choice you are about to make is conducive to that end, or whether it is an obstacle to it. If a father has not this object in view, if he consults only his son's temporal welfare, the son may be lead to eternal perdition by entering on a state of life chosen for him through such an improper motive. What will it then avail him to have enjoyed temporal prosperity and happiness for a few years? And even this cannot last for any length of time, for he only can enjoy true and permanent happiness who, following his vocation, leads a life pleasing to God.

You fail again in your choice of a state of life for your son when you do not consult his inclinations. If a certain inclination and love for a particular state of life is a good sign of a vocation to it, it is also an evidence that a person in such a state will be happy and contented, and will perform the duties and obligations of it. It is, therefore, in every case, dangerous to urge a son to enter into a state of life to which he has an aversion.

You err again in choosing a state of life for your son if you do not take into account his natural and acquired abilities and his corporal and mental qualifications. The son will then be placed in a position for which he has not the necessary qualifications, for which he has not and cannot acquire the necessary knowledge and skill; he cannot, therefore perform the duties of this state. This is a great misfortune to him and to others.

You fail again if you cannot answer satisfactorily the question whether the state of life chosen for your son affords sufficient security for his temporal welfare and happiness.

The more there is to be considered the more difficult it is to make a proper selection; and as the son's welfare for time and eternity depends on the selection of this state of life the greater is the responsibility of the father who makes the choice. It is indeed of so much importance as to cause him to seriously reflect on it, to take counsel, ask advice of experienced persons, to recommend the matter to God by fervent prayer, and beg the grace to know the true state of life to which his son is called, that he may not be led astray by improper motives, but that he may do that which is most pleasing to His divine majesty. "Show, O Lord, what thou hast chosen."

If the importance of this duty were well understood and well performed by Christian fathers how much misery and unhappiness would be spared to many a son! All would then enter into that state of life to which they are called, and with God's blessing they would enjoy true happiness.

We have now to add a few words in regard to the married state of life. We have in view more particularly the daughters, though what is to be said is also applicable to sons.

Worldly motives, temporal advantages, almost always prevail in the choice of the married state in life, particularly when there is a great fortune, great honors, and dignities to be gained. No question is then asked about the religious sentiment or moral conduct of the other party; the consent is given, and everything is hastened lest the marriage might not take place. And yet it may be well known, for instance, that the young man is a profligate, a libertine, that he cares nothing for religion and church, that he neglects his religious duties, that, in a word, he has fallen away from his faith and his Church and bears not a good name. And yet we deplore so many unhappy marriages!

Yes, your daughter has made a fine match; she is the lady of a noble house, the wife of a wealthy gentleman; she lives in grand style, she is honored and respected. But what kind of a husband has she? He is thoughtless, without religion, has no regard for virtue, follows his wicked inclinations, is unfaithful to his wife, wounds her feelings and causes her grief and sorrow. Mistress of such a beautiful house, dressed in costly garments, surrounded by servants, moving in the highest circles of society, this wife is unhappy, discontented, her heart consumed by grief. And will not this, your daughter, under such circumstances, become careless about spiritual and holy things? Will she not in the end lead a thoughtless and a sinful life? The children will follow the example of the father and mother. What hopes are there here for eternity? The present age affords numerous examples of what we have said. Yes, we have good reason to complain when we see parents so regardless of their duty in this particular while in other things they act as good Christians. They give their good and pious daughters away in marriage to young men such as we have described. Of course they flatter themselves with the hope that the young wife will, by her good example, convert her husband and bring him back to a better life. But, alas! how generally the contrary takes place. How often have such hopes proved to be mere castles in the air? The young wife, living in daily and intimate intercourse with her husband, will be drawn over to his way of thinking and living, and at last she and her children go with him to destruction.

It is then impossible for a truly Christian father to consent to such a marriage, no matter how great the temporal advantages of such a union may be; he will not sell his daughter's soul or her true happiness for the sake of a few temporal advantages.

Two Model Fathers.

I. Abraham.—Mixed Marriages.

THE last two subjects which we have treated of call to mind two model fathers, of whom the Holy Scriptures give us an account. The first is Abraham. He lived among a heathen and immoral people, and wishing to choose a wife for his son Isaac he was careful that none of the daughters of that people should become his son's wife, lest their evil example might lead him astray. He therefore sent the elder servant of his house, the faithful Eliezer, and commanded him to go to his (Abraham's) own country and kindred, and there select a virtuous wife for his son. And how earnestly did not Abraham devote himself to this duty! Eliezer was obliged to swear that he would faithfully execute the orders of his master. "Put thy hand under my thigh," said Abraham to him, "that I may make thee swear by the Lord, the God of heaven and earth, that thou take not a wife for my son of the daughters of the Chanaanites, among whom I dwell: but that thou go to my own country and kindred, and take a wife from thence for my son Isaac" (Gen. xxiv. 2, 3, 4). And Eliezer did as his master commanded him to do; he selected Batheul's daughter, the noble Rebecca, and God's blessing was on this union.

There is no doubt that among the daughters of the Chanaanites there were many remarkable for their beauty and other accomplishments, and possessed of great riches. An alliance with a daughter of the country in which he dwelt might have been of great advantage to Abraham; but he cared not for temporal gain, the honor of God and the spiritual welfare of his son was of more importance to him. His sole object was that his son should have a wife who feared the Lord and did his holy will.

Would to God that all fathers thought and acted thus! How much happier would the marriages of their children be for time and eternity!

These words of Abraham, "That thou take not a wife for my son of the daughters of the Chanaanites," are of very great importance, and should not be passed over without comment, as they have reference to mixed marriages. May we hope that every Christian father will in this matter follow the noble example of Abraham? It should be his principle never to consent that his son or daughter enter into a matrimonial alliance with a non-Catholic. A father whose heart clings to his faith and Church cannot be indifferent about the religious faith of those whom his son or daughter intend to take as partners for life for better or for worse. We regret that our limited space does not permit us to treat of this subject more at length; we will therefore confine ourselves to a few remarks.

There is certainly no more intimate relationship than that which exists between man and wife. "And they shall be two in one flesh." How intimately, then, should the hearts of man and wife be united! But can this be the case if there is no unity of feeling and sentiment in matters of religion, if they not only have not the same religious convictions, but, on the contrary, hold different and antagonistic doctrines? Real and true conjugal happiness can never be enjoyed in such mixed marriages. If the married couple are both indifferent to religion and faith their life will not be disturbed by differences of religious belief, but they cannot enjoy true and permanent conjugal happiness, for this is only possible where there is religion and faith. The difference in religion, then, even when neither man nor wife is particularly devoted to his or her particular faith, will yet more or less disturb the peace of their hearts. Habits, customs, associations, and relationships constantly clash and create a cause of permanent discontent and dissatisfaction. If a father, then, thinks to benefit his child by consenting to a mixed marriage because of the promise of temporal advantages he is greatly mistaken. The anticipated happiness is a delusion. And it must not be forgotten that the non-Catholic party may sooner or later make use of the supposed right of divorce and marry another. Will not the mere possibility of this make the Catholic party very unhappy?

But this is not the greatest danger arising from mixed marriages. The Catholic party and his or her children run a great risk, for such marriages are dangerous to their spiritual welfare.

How easy for the Catholic party to lose that lively faith and Catholic spirit which animates his or her bosom, and to grow careless in the practices of the faith when the non-Catholic party looks on them with contempt, and ridicules and laughs at them! He who understands the instability of the human will and the weakness of the human heart will readily admit that there is, under such circumstances, great danger of growing lukewarm and indifferent and finally losing the faith.

But what can we think of mixed marriages when we reflect on the fate of the children! We assume as a matter of course that there was before the marriage an understanding or contract that all the children must be brought up in the Catholic faith. Without an understanding of this kind such marriages are not permitted; the Church has strictly forbidden them. But after all, is this promise, so solemnly made—

granting its sincerity—a sufficient security that the children will be brought up in the Catholic faith? What if the non-Catholic party, influenced by friends and relations, should prove unfaithful to the promise given? Such cases are not rare. Or what if circumstances compel a removal to a non-Catholic neighborhood, where there is no church, no priest, no Catholic school? Or the Catholic party may die and the children be left to the non-Catholic party, who may very probably marry again, and a Protestant at that. How then can the children receive a good Catholic education?

Alas, how sad, in most cases, is the fate of those poor children born of mixed marriages! And what a responsibility rests on him who, through negligence or carelessness, has been the cause of such sad consequences? Perhaps the parents of those who have contracted mixed marriages are most to blame, in as much as they did not do their duty and try to prevent such marriages. What a judgment awaits them!

But even in the most favorable cases, where there is no obstacle to prevent the children from being brought up in the Catholic faith, still the Catholic education of such children cannot be called perfect. We have frequently remarked that if the education of the children is to be conducted according to the will of God the father and mother must unite in the work and lead them by word and example to be Christian men and women. Now even if the Catholic party be animated by the faith and the Catholic spirit (which, however, in mixed marriages is very rarely the case) yet there can be no Catholic education worth mentioning. It is a matter of halves, and one half of the teaching faculty is wanting. The Protestant does not and cannot contribute to the education of the Catholic child. The education is therefore imperfect.

But how will it be with the education of the Catholic child when it is confided to the care of a Protestant mother? Its mind is formed from infancy, and impressions made in infancy remain in after life. But how can this non-Catholic mother infuse a Catholic spirit into her child, even if she would? The example of parents has much to do in the education of the children, hence what a great disadvantage to a child when its mother is wanting in this most important point—practice of the true faith? Besides, what impression is made on the heart of the child when it sees its father or mother so careless in those things which it is taught to consider of so much importance, and when it sees that what is dear to the Catholic heart is looked upon as superstition by the non-Catholic parent?

A true Catholic education is impossible in mixed marriages, and thus the child is deprived of that which is most important to its salvation.

You cannot appeal to the fact that the Church grants dispensations in certain cases and under certain conditions The Church positively disapproves of such unions; and if in certain cases she does not prevent them or appears in a way to countenance them she does so with a heavy heart and to avoid a greater evil, for she holds such marriages to be evil. This follows from the nature of the case. For how can a person who is animated by a true Catholic spirit enter into such a union without having the most grave reasons, when he knows that the person with whom he is united by the bonds of marriage does not agree with him in that which he considers of the greatest importance? A true Catholic struggles against it, but if he have not these sentiments it is a sign that he is already perverted, and in mixed marriages such perversion will increase.

For this reason, then, a Christian father will always discountenance mixed marriages and use his influence to prevent them.

II. Tobias.

Tobias is a beautiful companion picture to the great patriarch Abraham. Being a captive in Assyria he was compelled to send his son, the younger Tobias, to Gabelus, who dwelt in the city of Rages, in the land of the Medes. But how careful he was to procure a trustworthy guide, who might advise and protect him on his long journey. "Go now," said he to his son, "and seek thee out some faithful man to go with thee" (Tob. v. 4). Tobias was a man of prayer, and whilst his son was obeying his order he undoubtedly prayed that the Lord might send him a good guide. We know how God sent the angel Raphael to be the guardian of the son of his faithful servant. When the angel approached him under the appearance of a young man Tobias said, "Canst thou conduct my son to Gabelus at Rages, a city of the Medes? and when thou shalt return I will pay thee thy hire." Then he dismissed the travellers, saying: "May you have a good journey, and God be with you in your way and his Angel accompany you." And when they had departed and the mother began to weep he consoled her with these prophetic words: "Weep not, our son will arrive thither safe, and will return safe to us; and thy eyes shall see him. For I believe that the good Angel of God doth accompany him and doth order all things well that are done, so that he shall return to us with joy." We know that his hope was verified.

This beautiful history shows also that God himself will take good care of the children of pious parents when they recommend them to his protection, especially if circumstances compel them to be absent from home. When therefore a Christian father and mother do their best to render the situation of their children safe, and do not fail to pray for them, the Lord will take charge of them and protect them, though not in such a wonderful manner as he did Tobias. "For he hath given his angels charge over thee: to keep thee in thy ways: in their hands they shall bear thee up; lest thou dash thy foot against a stone" (Psalm xc. 11, 12).

Inasmuch as we have made mention of this most excellent father, who is in every respect a most admirable model for every man and father of a family, we advise every father to read the Book of Tobias. We cannot deny ourselves the pleasure of copying the fourth chapter of this history. It contains those beautiful admonitions which

Tobias gave his son when he thought that the end of life was near at hand. "Hear, my son, the words of my mouth, and lay them as a foundation in thy heart. When God shall take my soul, thou shalt bury my body; and thou shalt honor thy mother all the days of her life: for thou must be mindful what and how great perils she suffered for thee in her womb. And when she also shall have ended the time of her life, bury her by me. And all the days of thy life have God in thy mind: and take heed thou never consent to sin, nor transgress the commandments of the Lord our God. Give alms out of thy substance, and turn not away thy face from any poor person: for so it shall come to pass that the face of the Lord shall not be turned from thee. According to thy ability be merciful. If thou have much, give abundantly; if thou have little, take care even so to bestow willingly a little; for thus thou storest up to thyself a good reward for the day of necessity. For alms deliver from all sin, and from death, and will not suffer the soul to go into darkness. Alms shall be a great confidence before the most high God, to all them that give it. Take heed to keep thyself, my son, from all fornication, and beside thy wife never endure to know a crime. Never suffer pride to reign in thy mind, or in thy words: for from it all perdition took its beginning. If any man hath done any work for thee, immediately pay him his hire: and let not the wages of thy hired servant stay with thee at all. See thou never do to another what thou wouldst hate to have done to thee by another. Eat thy bread with the hungry and the needy; and with thy garments cover the naked. Lay out thy bread and thy wine upon the burial of a just man; and do not eat and drink thereof with the wicked. Seek counsel always of a wise man.

Bless God at all times, and desire of him to direct thy ways, and that all thy counsels may abide in him. Fear not, my son; we lead indeed a poor life, but we shall have many good things if we fear God, and depart from all sin and do that which is good" (Tob. iv.).

The Farmer of Münster.

THE *Missionsblatt* for 1852 gave a series of interesting contributions under the title of "The Red Farmer." The subject of these sketches was a most excellent farmer in Münster, province of Westphalia, whom the young people called "The Red Farmer," on account of an old-fashioned red coat in which he used to appear in town and at church. Many good and beautiful things are told of him in these sketches, which were written by his son, a priest, who speaks of his excellent father as follows:

"He was a good educator, although he followed only his own good common-sense, and had never in his life read a book on education. I was of a quick, excitable nature, and easily carried away by impulse. But my father knew how to curb my impulses and render me tractable by various humiliations. When I quarrelled with a servant or with any of my three brothers I would have to be the first to offer the hand of reconciliation if I would not fall under his displeasure, which I feared above all things. If I was angry about something and would neither eat nor speak, a strict order was given that no one should pay any attention to me. None should ask me what was the matter; none should ask me to eat; they were to leave me entirely alone, and not trouble themselves about me. This was an intolerable punishment, and I soon began to repent of my anger and stubbornness.

"He scarcely ever had recourse to corporal punishment. He punished me as often as possible through myself by opposing me with the opposite of the fault by which I had offended. I was once sitting at the fire when he came home from the field; a young colt had been harnessed to be taught to work. My father thought I would be delighted to see them taming the spirited animal, and therefore invited me to go with him. But I was in an ill-humor because my mother gave me only a very small piece of bread and butter, and I replied that I did not want to go out. My father noticed my obstinacy and replied: 'Well, then, if you do not want to accompany me you can stay where you are.' I was soon after punished for not complying with his wish, as some hot water from the kettle spilled on my foot. But this was not all; in the afternoon I was anxious to go into the garden and get some pears. I asked my father, who was cleaning seed corn in the kitchen, if he would go with me and knock the pears from the tall pear tree in the garden. He answered: 'I could easily spare the time, but at present I care as little to go out with you as you did this morning when I asked you to go out with me.' Thus he showed me how petty and contemptible my stubbornness was.

"Another time I was playing in the barn. My father came with the keys to fasten the doors, but I did not want to go out, and begged him to go away again and not spoil my fun. He gave me the reason why he wanted to close the doors just then and asked me again to come out. I did not regard the reasons and repeated my request to stay. What did he do? He shut the doors and left me there till evening without food or drink. At first it was not at all unpleasant, and I continued my sport. But after an hour, when the bell on the roof of the house called the folks to supper and I was terrified at the moaning of the wind, I became restless and tried to get out. But in spite of all my efforts I could scarcely move the heavy doors, much less open them. My cries frightened a great owl that with loud hoot and clatter flew out from under the roof. No one paid any attention to the little prisoner. Night was coming on and no rescuer appeared. My repentance through anxiety and terror reached the highest grade. Then, for the first time in my life, I learned to pray from my heart. I went on my knees and recited all the prayers I knew. At last my father came and opened the door. When I promised not to go against his will again he remained silent.

"He seldom censured or blamed, and seldom resorted to positive punishment. He punished me through myself. He was accustomed in the long winter evenings to hold a kind of school. Once I showed reluctance to go into the room, and declared openly that I would rather remain with the servants and help cut turnips for the cattle. My two sisters followed my father very willingly. After a time I heard singing in the room. My father was teaching them the song 'Prince Eugene, the Noble Knight,' etc. I threw aside the knife with which I was cutting turnips, took my books and inkstand, and hastened to the room. It was locked, and I could not join in the amusements of the others. I sat down sadly on the step and bewailed my fault. But when the others came out and showed me the beautiful picture-book which my father had brought home from town that afternoon and given to them for their willingness to learn I almost died of sorrow. Thus was my self-will severely punished, and yet without the rod.

"While he did not let my faults go unpunished he knew how to suitably reward me when I deserved it. When I had for several days distinguished myself by obedience and diligence I would know without being told why I received the reward which he gave in such a pleasant, kindly manner. To know that father was pleased with us was the sweetest of all rewards. At noon and in the evening he made, very cleverly too, all kinds of toys for us. Once he made a little wagon and harness so that we could make the big dog draw us about; another time he made a fiddle, with which we amused ourselves. For my sisters he made work-boxes, needle-cases, and cradles for their dolls. While he was thus employed we made ourselves busy holding the boards, etc., and giving our opinion as to the way in which the playthings ought to be made. He would always answer kindly our countless questions. If we pleased him we could stay with him while thus employed, but whoever fell under his displeasure received the order to go away and do some work elsewhere.

And when all three of us had in any manner offended him then the work intended for our amusement was immediately stopped. He would treat us coldly, scarcely look at us, and appear as if he did not care for us. It is now thirty years since then, yet I can recall to mind how happy we were when our conduct met his approval, and how miserable we felt when through some fault we had lost his love and friendship.

"Every Sunday afternoon we had to give an account of our work at school by showing our lessons and copy-books. If the teacher came to our house we had to go and meet him in a friendly manner and invite and accompany him into the room, when a strict investigation of our lessons and conduct would take place. Only then could we retire. When our parents showed great love and respect for the teacher it increased our esteem for him.

"When I studied later at the gymnasium he continued the same strict control. When I came home in vacation I would be asked, even before I got my pack off my back, 'Well, where is your testimonial? Let us see how it looks.' I drew forth my report, which he examined with the greatest care and compared with the previous one, of which he kept a copy. If my progress was satisfactory he rejoiced exceedingly. Once I came home with a heavy heart, for my report began thus: 'Conduct: good, but the pupil was punished once for an error.' With a trembling hand I reached it to my strict judge, for I feared to be sent back again. Fortunately he made a mistake in reading it. Instead of reading, 'Punished *for* an error,' he read, 'Punished *through* an error,' and he considered this an apology on the part of the teacher for having punished me by mistake; and so I came well out of it. My teacher had long observed my reverence and awe for my father, and he knew well how to use them for my benefit by threatening to inform him if I was negligent or remiss. All other punishments were as nothing to me in comparison with this threat. Even after my father's death this awe of him saved me in danger of sin when I remembered that he, in heaven, knew my conduct.

"My father's favorite recreation was to play with us children at noon and in the evening. Nuremberg toys were unknown to us, but we had our wooden horse, our wagon, our swings and see-saws, our bows and arrows, as well as the town children. My father took great pleasure in making these toys for us.

"Every Sunday afternoon when the weather was fine we went with him and mother walking in the woods and fields.

We used to call it 'going around.' How our little dog with his red collar ran hither and thither, while our paents followed us and took pleasure in answering our thousand questions! We then learned to observe not only the birds and flowers, but also the goodness and love of God in the waving grain. 'Father,' I once asked on one of these walks, 'why does God make the stalk so slender that it can scarcely support the heavy ear?' He answered: 'Do you see that little bird? Now look; it tries to pick grain out of the ear, but when it lights on the stalk it bends down and its attempts are in vain.' 'Yes, yes; I now see that God has ordered it wisely. The bean-stalk can be thicker, because the birds cannot swallow the beans,' I answered.

"In like manner he taught us to admire the wisdom of God in the notches and joints of the stem, in the covering of the kernel, and in a thousand other things in nature. This afforded me great pleasure, which he would still more increase to my advantage. 'Tell me, my child,' said he, 'why are you so glad?' I answered, 'It is such a beautiful day that the birds are glad, and why should I not be glad? We will have a good harvest, and plenty to eat, and some to divide with the poor. That is why I am glad. On every flower, on every stalk, on every ear shines the goodness and wisdom of God, as you taught me. Father, since it is so beautiful here, how much more beautiful will it be in heaven.' Conversing thus together we came to the end of the field and sat down on the trunk of a tree, when my father taught me this prayer: 'To serve thee, O Lord, is happiness: to live according to thy will causes greater joy and contentedness than all the gold and riches of the world.'

"If after the usual family devotions

there was time, we all, young and old, would have a game of some kind, generally a game of ball. At the father's word, 'Enough for to-day,' the play was at an end.

"Easter eve was the happiest time in my life. For two weeks previous we were busy gathering wood, briars, and straw, to have all ready for Easter Sunday. After having eaten our Easter eggs we would leave the house, my father with his prayer- and hymn-book, I with the pan of fire, the hired man with the pitchfork, and even the stable-boy was not absent on this occasion. He would bring up the rear of the procession dragging a long bean-pole after him, to add his share to the solemnity of the day by vigorously poking the fire to make the flame blaze up high, so that his companions on the next day could not make fun of him on the way to school. As soon as the fire was kindled we all marched around it, and father would start the hymn, 'Christ is Risen,' and other hymns, which we would all sing. You, dear reader, should have been there to have an idea of our joy and devotion. I have never in after life celebrated Easter without recalling to mind the joy and happiness I then felt, and wishing I could enjoy them once again.

"As much as my father encouraged proper amusements and entertainments, and would prepare them for the members of his household, knowing that man needs them, yet he was not a friend of certain amusements that were customary at weddings, dancing parties, and carnivals. And though he was of the opinion that even the best regulated dancing parties did not amount to much he never condemned them indiscriminately. He preferred to take measures to lessen as far as possible the dangers which more or less accompany such entertainments, and gradually do away with them **altogether.**"

Let us now hear something of the religious life of this excellent father. His son, the priest, thus continues the narrative:

"In his bed-room was a clean white table, upon which stood a large crucifix which he had brought with him from Kevelaer. There was no kneeling-bench in front of the table, for he would kneel on the bare floor. Here he would pray for at least a quarter of an hour after having said night prayers with the members of the household in the kitchen, though tired and weary after the day's work. In his prayers for others he in a special manner prayed for the parish, the welfare of which he had much at heart. His manner of praying was, like himself, natural and unaffected, and when at his devotions he was so absorbed in meditation that nothing could disturb him. He had his bed-room adorned with valuable steel engravings which he had received as memorials from the five former pastors of the parish, whom he had outlived. A small holy-water font and two much used but well preserved rosaries hung against the wall; those beads, he said, were about one hundred years old.

"He received holy communion on the four great feasts of the year and on the festivals of the Blessed Virgin, so that he received about every six weeks. He prepared himself not only by fervent prayer, but he would on such occasions give more than his usual alms to some needy family or hand it to the pastor for distribution. He made two pilgrimages every year; one to the holy cross at Cresfeld, the other to Kevelaer. To persons who did not believe in pilgrimages he would say: 'I am entirely of your opinion, that we can pray as well here as in any other place; but if we remain here we will not do it. In my younger days I also repeated the stupid proverb: People who do not want to work at home go to Holland to work, and those who do not want to pray at home go to Kevelaer to pray. But after I had been once at that holy place I was ashamed to have been so narrow-minded as to have said anything against so holy a practice.' He saw with great joy the revival of this devout practice among Catholics."*

---

* It is interesting to know that this worthy man was as excellent a farmer as he was a Christian, thus refuting those who think that true piety is incompatible with good business habits. He did not believe in following every whim of fashion, but as far as agriculture was concerned he was in favor of progress. He attended regularly the weekly meetings of an agricultural society of which he was a member, and adopted the methods recommended by it. Many sneered at his attempts and experiments, but only to imitate his example afterwards.

A word or two in conclusion about his last

moments. After having made his last will and testament he said: "Children, it is all over now; a few days more and you will carry me away. Pray for my poor soul." To his son, who was preparing for the priesthood (the writer of the above sketch), he said, among other things: "Son, strive to follow the vocation you have freely chosen; honor your mother, and help your sisters by wise counsel." In his address at the funeral the parish priest said: "We stand at the grave of a man of honor, whom I loved as a father; following good, time-honored customs, he gained by his example of moderation, temperance, justice, and purity the respect and veneration of all who knew him. Would that I were as sure of the eternal crown of happiness as he is. None of you who now stand at his grave could help honoring and respecting the deceased, and many of you are under great obligations to him."

The Father at Prayer.

WE cannot close our remarks on "The Christian Father" without adding a few words about prayer. Prayer is one of those necessary requisites which belong to the vocation of a father; to be a truly Christian father he must be a man of prayer.

If we could suppose that our little book "The Christian Mother" (which we have spoken of above) would be read by Christian fathers we might simply refer them to page 145 of that book, where we treat of this subject, and it is as applicable to fathers as to mothers. But as we cannot depend on this chance, and as it is a matter of great importance which fathers should seriously take to heart, it will not be amiss to treat briefly of the subject here.

Those who have even a slight knowledge of the vocation of a father will admit that it is a difficult one, and that its duties cannot be faithfully performed without special assistance from above. The father needs this assistance to know how to bring up his children properly, and the children are in need of it that the father's efforts in their behalf may bear fruit. But to obtain this assistance the father must pray.

He must pray for himself that the Lord may assist him to be a good father to his children. He must pray for the grace to lead a good Christian life, to avoid this or that sin, to fulfil his obligations, for all this is necessary to a successful bringing up of children. He must also, like the mother, pray to God for good and sound judgment and discernment, that in difficult cases he may determine the true course to be taken; that he may know how to treat his children, each according to his or her disposition, ability, good or bad qualities. He must pray for the real supernatural love for his children, and for the grace of perseverance under the many difficulties he may meet with and the sacrifices he has to make in the education of his children. Can a father be found who, understanding the great importance of a good education and realizing the difficulties connected with it, will not feel inclined to ask assistance and help of God?

He must pray for his children. The more he loves them and wishes to lead them to their true welfare the more fervently will he pray for them. For no matter how much he may have done for them he must remember that his efforts will not bear fruit unless the Lord mercifully grants his grace and assistance. He will therefore always pray for them. Can we suppose that a good father could say his morning and evening prayers, receive holy communion, etc., without remembering his children?

He recommends to God in prayer whatever he does for his children. He prays that the Lord may preserve them in his divine grace and enable them to overcome their evil inclinations; he prays that God may assist them to advance in the Christian virtues, and lead them to eternal happiness.

A Christian father will pray for his child when it goes to confession and holy communion; in a special manner will he pray for it when it leaves home to live among strangers. The greater the dangers to son or daughter the more fervent will be the father's prayers. Or it may be a question as to a choice of a state of life; how important then that he should pray that their choice may be according to the most holy will of God. Again, the children may be addicted to certain vicious habits; the son or daughter has been led astray; they heed not his advice, care not for his admonitions, and even punishment is of no avail. The father's heart bleeds, but he cannot remedy the evil. One thing alone remains to him, he has recourse to prayer. He prays for his unhappy child, and quits not till his prayer is granted.

There are innumerable occasions on which a father is called upon to pray, and a Christian father obeys the call. In all his prayers he remembers his children, and the greater the necessity the more fervently will he pray. In his prayers he will address Jesus, the true friend of children. He will invoke in their behalf the intercession of the Blessed Virgin, of the angels, patron saints, and all the saints in heaven.

The child of such a father is indeed happy; by his prayers he calls down upon the child the gifts and graces of God. And however great the blessings may be which the child has derived from a Christian education the father's prayers are still a greater blessing, for all else that he does for his child receives from his prayers its power and efficacy.

Happy is the child who has a father (and mother) who pray for their children! A father and mother praying for their children—that is a spectacle on which the eyes of God love to dwell, and their united prayer is an appeal which he must answer. We therefore repeat here: "Oh, fathers, pray; pray without ceasing; pray with fervor and from your heart for your children!"

PART II.

Prayers for a Christian Father.

It is a beautiful and commendable practice, to read in the afternoons of Sundays, if it be only during the devotion—but not during the prayers, that may perhaps be said in common—one of the chapters of the first part, either entirely or partly. By this, what has been said would always be called to mind.

Prayers.
A Prayer for Piety and the Fear of God.

O GOD, thou hast brought me into being solely that during my short life here on earth I may, by fulfilling thy holy will, save my soul and thus glorify thy holy name for all eternity. I can be truly happy here on earth only when, in view of this end, I lead a life according to thy holy will. I also am a father. Thou hast intrusted children to me, to bring them up for thee, and lead them in thy fear to a Christian life. Woe is me if I do not correspond to thy beneficent designs! How great is the responsibility, how terrible the punishment! And yet I cannot bring up my children in thy holy fear and to a pious life if I myself am not animated by true piety and the fear of God. O God, grant me the grace to have this great truth always before my eyes. Arouse me by it and help me to lay it more than all else to heart, that I may lead a life agreeable to thee, that I may be a good father to my children and save my soul. Grant me grace to avoid and flee from all that hinders or endangers a Christian life; teach me to do conscientiously all that is necessary and useful to continue in the way of salvation. O ye elect, ye fathers who are in heaven! pray for me. Amen.

A Prayer for the Grace of Faith.

O God, who hast by thy unbegotten Son revealed those truths and teachings which are necessary or conducive to our salvation, and proclaimed them to us by thy holy, infallible Church, increase in me the grace of faith, that I may accept these lessons of salvation with undoubting confidence. When, through the suggestions of my proud nature and through the conversations and example of an unbelieving world, I am in danger of wavering in my faith, guide and direct me; teach me to understand that our holy faith rests on firm foundations, and that only a perverse heart can doubt. Teach me how to guard the precious treasure of faith with scrupulous watchfulness, and avoid reading all writings dangerous to faith, or to unnecessarily associate with men who have suffered shipwreck of their faith, that I may not suffer a like loss. Above all, O Lord, assist me to live according to the holy faith, and order my life according to thy teachings; then through thy grace will the light of faith shine brighter and brighter, and fill my heart with confidence.

I also recommend to thee my children; protect them in the dangers to their holy faith; may they, through thy grace, be steadfast and true children of the Church, and hold firmly her teachings. Amen.

A Prayer to obtain the Virtue of Temperance.

O God, who through thy divine Son and through thy servants hast so strongly warned us against intemperance and drunkenness, and who willest that we as Christians "walk not in rioting," but as followers of Jesus and his mortified life, grant me the grace of true Christian moderation. Prevent me from ever becoming a victim of the fatal vice of drunkenness. Alas, if my children should have the reproach of having a drunken father! O Lord, fill me with horror of this vice, that I may not expose myself to its dangers, and become a drunkard. Grant that I may never overstep the bounds of Christian moderation, but that I may remain true to its holy injunctions. Teach me to avoid all unnecessary visits to public-houses, and to avoid association with frivolous persons. Protect me with thy strong arm, O Lord, amid the many dangers of this pleasure-seeking age, and grant me the spirit of moderation and sobriety. Amen.

A Prayer against Inordinate Love of the World.

O divine Saviour, who admonishest us that "we must seek first the kingdom of God and his justice," may I ever obey thy admonition! Alas! I am so easily carried away by my earthly occupations, that I totally forget thee, and, neglecting prayer and other pious exercises, become more and more estranged from thee and heavenly things. Can I hope to participate in those heavenly treasures to which I am now so indifferent? Must I not fear that my inordinate, worldly manner of life may cause me the loss of my soul. Then woe is me when I must at last acknowledge how unreasonable I was to devote my whole life and strength to things of which I am so easily deprived by death, and to neglect those things which could render me eternally happy! Tear then, O Lord, from my heart by thy grace the love of earthly things! Grant that I may understand that all earthly efforts and occupations are only the means by which to serve thee and acquire merits for eternity. Grant that all my actions may be done with a good intention. Give me fervor in prayer and spiritual exercises, that I may never neglect my daily devotions, that Sundays and holy days be holy in my sight; on them I will take the prescribed rest that I may devote myself to prayer, and assist at the solemnities of the Church. Preserve me, O Lord, from negligence in the reception of the holy sacraments by which I receive strength and grace. Awake me in time and lead me to the banquet of salvation. Assist me then, O Lord, that I may so use the things of this world as not to lose the things of eternity. Amen.

A Prayer on the Anniversary of Marriage.*

O my God and Lord, it was on this day that in thy holy house, kneeling at the foot of the altar, I received the holy sacrament of matrimony and entered with its blessing into the marriage state. Can I let it pass without thanksgiving and gratitude to thee? No, O

---

* Good Christians thus happily united should approach together the sacraments, either on the anniversary of their marriage or on the Sunday preceding or following it, in order to receive them with better preparation, and to renew the graces of the sacrament of matrimony. What a beautiful practice! Could not married people at least assist at Mass with this intention? Do they realize how much they stand in need of the blessing and assistance of God in the midst of so many important duties, surrounded as they are by so many difficulties and dangers, that they may not perish, but work out their salvation? It was for this very reason that our Lord instituted the sacrament of matrimony, and this same reason shows also how commendable a practice it is to renew yearly the graces received in this Sacrament.

Lord, from my whole heart I thank thee for having lead me through thy sacrament into the married state, sanctified my matrimonial union, and opened the treasures of thy grace to me, that I might be enabled to correspond with the requirements of my state of life, and to persevere in fidelity and love towards my wife, in conjugal purity, and to bring up my children in thy fear, and thus to work out my salvation. I thank thee for every grace which in virtue of this sacrament I have since received; I thank thee for thy protection and assistance, and for all good which thou hast granted me and mine. Praise be to thee for all eternity!

But have I, in co-operation with thy grace, fulfilled the obligations of my state? Have I lived as a truly Christian father and husband? Alas, I have much to accuse myself of. O my God, I am most heartily sorry. Have pity on me! Forgive me in thy infinite mercy and for the sake of thy Son, Jesus! I am firmly resolved: I will in future strive with renewed fervor to fulfil faithfully and conscientiously every duty as a Christian and a father. How can I otherwise hope to be in thy grace and gain salvation? But, O Lord, of what avail are all my resolutions, if thou dost not give the grace to keep them? Renew then, O Lord, on this day the blessing of the sacrament, and grant that its grace may day by day abundantly flow into my heart; animated and strengthened by it, I will be mindful and able to perform the duties of my vocation.

For my wife also I beseech thy favor and grace. Grant that we, so intimately united by thy sacrament, may always be in the love and fear of God, that our married life be, as it should, an image of the intimate union of Christ with his holy Church, and lead us to eternal life.

Remember also, O Lord, the children thou hast given us. Bless them, protect them, grant them grace that they may live according to thy will. Assist me that I may bring them up entirely for thee.

Holy Virgin and Mother Mary, St. Joseph and all the saints who have lived in the married state, pray for me. Amen.

Morning Prayer.

O Lord, thou hast granted me this day, that by fulfilling my duties to thee I may work out my salvation. Assist me then with thy grace. Grant above all that I may fulfil the most important and holy duties, my duties towards my children, and that in particular I may afford them a good example. Bless all that I may say or do this day for their instruction and edification.

And my children, O Lord, take them under the protection of thy love and grace; guard them in dangers, and protect them from all evil. Preserve them from sin; fill their young hearts with thy holy love; animate and strengthen them with thy grace, that they may serve thee faithfully, and that as they increase in age they may increase in virtue and grace.

Ye guardian angels and patrons of my children, I commend them to you; take charge of them and pray for them. Amen.

Evening Prayer.*

Thanks be to thee, O God and Father, for all the graces and favors which thou

---

* Do not omit, Christian father, to examine your conscience in the evening, if it be only for some minutes, especially whether you have faithfully performed your duties during the day. Was your example such as to be worthy of imitation? Have you said or done anything that could have given scandal to your children? Have you had as careful an eye over your children as you should have had? Have you permitted them to rove about unguarded? Have you brought them to church, to school? Did hast this day bestowed on me and on my children. All good gifts come from thee. Thou rulest over us mercifully. Alas that I have been so ungrateful, and have offended thee the best of fathers! Pardon mercifully! Forgive me my neglects of the duties of my vocation... What can I do but beseech thy grace? Be gracious to me! May I still more and more understand the sacredness of my paternal duties, and fulfil

---

you take it to heart to give them useful instruction; to remind them of God, and of higher things? Have you reminded them of their faults? Have you admonished, warned, and punished them according to duty? Have you, in doing this, given way to anger and impatience, and punished them beyond measure? Have you taught them to say their prayers and insisted on their doing so; on their loving God and man; on their being truthful, obedient, peaceable, industrious, lovers of cleanliness and order? Do you pray for them as you should? Be sorry if you have committed faults; ask God's pardon, resolve and promise our Lord to be more faithful on the morrow.

them! Yes, O Lord, it is my firm purpose. I promise thee anew. Come with thy precious grace to my assistance; inflame my heart evermore with thy holy love and with love for my children, that filled with holy fervor I may bring them up for thee and for eternal life.

For this night, O Lord, I commend them to thee. May thy hand protect them in their nightly rest; drive away the enemy from their place of sleep; may thy holy angel be near them. O do not permit that night may be an occasion of sin to them; preserve them in innocence and in immaculate purity!

Holy Virgin, St. Joseph, ye holy angels and elect, I commend my children to thy care. Amen.

Prayers at Mass for a Christian Father.

AT THE INTROIT.

O Lord, I come here into thy holy temple to implore grace for my state of life. I am not able to fulfil the duties of my vocation as thou willest, if thou wilt not grant me thy assistance. Thou hast assured me of the help of thy grace in the holy sacrament of marriage. Would that I were worthy of it. Alas, I confess my unworthiness, and that I am not deserving of thy grace. Therefore do I come to the altar of thy divine Son, that united with the holy sacrifice which he consummates for me I may not appear unworthy, and find a hearing when I implore thy divine assistance and grace for my children. Grant then that I may assist at this holy sacrifice with devotion. Amen.

AT THE OFFERTORY.

O almighty and eternal God, in union with the priest, I also consecrate to thee this gift of bread and wine, and with him lay in spirit upon the altar the solicitude of my heart, my desire and prayer for grace to fulfil the duties of my state. O Lord, I acknowledge that my prayers, like the gift of bread and wine, are valueless; but as through thy goodness and power the bread and wine are changed into the sacrifice of the body and blood of thy divine Son, a sacrifice infinitely pleasing to thee, so grant in union with this holy sacrifice my petition to find grace in thy sight. I implore thee therefore in the spirit of humility, with contrite heart, and under the invocation of the most holy Virgin Mary, of St. Joseph, of all fathers who are in heaven, and of all the saints.

AT THE CONSECRATION.

O Jesus, thou deignest with infinite love to come down upon the altar at the word of thy servant to renew, under the form of bread and wine, the merciful sacrifice which was consummated on Golgotha, that we may participate in its graces.

In deepest humility I adore thee here present as my Lord and Saviour; praise and thanksgiving to thee from the bottom of my heart for so many graces. Receive me then, O Jesus, with my petition, in thy holy sacrifice. Grant my prayer that I may be a good father to my children, thy little ones. Amen.

AFTER THE CONSECRATION.

O God, my heart is now raised in trust and confidence to thee, for it is thy divine Son who represents me before thee, and presents my petition together with the sacrifice of his sacred body and blood. It is the same sacrifice which he once consummated on the cross in obedience to thy will. May my petition then, in union with this holy sacrifice and for his sake, find grace with thee. Pardon me then for any neglect of the duties of my calling; animate me that I may henceforth fulfil them with renewed zeal. Grant me all those graces which I stand in need of for the education of my children, an exemplary life, charity, wisdom, patience, mildness, perseverance, and fervor in prayer for my children. Grant me, O Lord, thy grace.

BEFORE AND AT COMMUNION.

Say the prayer to Jesus the friend of children, on p. 256.

AT THE END OF MASS.

See prayers on pp. 237 to 241.

A Prayer for Wisdom.

How great, O God, and how momentous is the vocation thou hast given me, and how difficult to fulfil it! I must bring up the children whom thou hast entrusted to me, and teach them to conquer their defects and practise the Christian virtues. O my God, I am ignorant and incompetent. How shall I always know the right way if thou dost not help me? Send, therefore, O Lord, from thy heavenly throne a ray of divine wisdom into my heart, as thou gavest to Solomon a wise, discerning heart, that he might rule his people well. Enlighten me that

I may know how to treat my children, each according to his way, that they may be freed from their failings and preserved from everything that is hurtful and dangerous to them; show me the means and the way to bring them up properly; lead me that I may be as far from dangerous forbearance as from unreasonable severity; give me the right word when I instruct, reprove, or admonish them. Make known to me thy holy will when I have to advise them. Led by thy hand, let me accomplish the work of their education; for thou ever leadest thy children with infinite wisdom in the way of salvation.

O Holy Ghost, thou dispenser of gifts and graces, grant me the gift of wisdom and of counsel, for the good of my children. Amen.—Our Father and Hail Mary.

A Prayer for Mildness.

Divine Saviour, who didst dwell for three years among thy disciples, as a father among his children, how much hadst thou to suffer from their imperfections and failings; how calculated was often their conduct to excite impatience and anger? And yet thou wast always so indulgent to them, so kind, so mild! An unfriendly, hard, cruel word never passed thy lips. Oh may I be like to thee in my demeanor towards my children! I must, if I am thy disciple, and wish to save my soul. May I then "learn from thee to be meek." When the misconduct of my children causes impatience and anger in me help me to overcome these emotions, that I may not manifest them. Grant that I may be calm and dispassionate in correcting or punishing my children. For "the anger of man worketh not the justice of God." O meek Jesus, have mercy on me! Amen.—Our Father and Hail Mary.

Prayer to Jesus, the Friend of Children.

O Jesus, how great was once thy love for children. It is still the same to-day. Yes, thy love for Christian children is still greater. And thou lovest, O divine Lord, my children more than I, and art their divine friend. Oh how consoling and encouraging for me! Praise be to thee! Grant me, then, the grace, O divine Saviour, that I may conduct myself towards my children according to thy will and pleasure. Grant that I may bring them up entirely for thee and lead them with all my strength to know thee more and more, to love thee, and to regulate their whole lives according to thy holy example, that they may become thy disciples and through thee obtain salvation. O Jesus, in virtue of the holy sacrament through which thou hast led me to the married state and the office of father, and by the grace of the holy sacrifice, assist me that I may fulfil all the obligations of a Christian father most faithfully and zealously. Let my life be a model for my children; fill my heart with that love which thy divine heart has for my children; give me wisdom, courage, patience, and meekness; give me fervor in my prayers for my children. May thy blessing be on all that I do for my children. Amen.

A Prayer to the Blessed Virgin.

O most blessed Virgin Mary, admirable Mother, since I have been found worthy to be a father I fly to thee. Pray for me, O holy and powerful Mother, that I may show myself worthy of my calling. May it be granted to me through thy powerful intercession that I may in future fulfil all duties as a Christian father conscientiously, faithfully, and perseveringly. What a holy and meritorious life thou didst lead, O holy Mother, by the side of thy spouse, with Jesus thy divine Son, in prayer and labor and good works, in the cottage at Nazareth! Oh let it be the model of my family life! Call down upon my household the spirit of piety and the fear of the Lord, that my children may prosper in all things. Amen.

A Prayer to St. Joseph.

O holy Joseph, thou faithful companion of the blessed Mother, thou who didst protect her and her divine child with such care, and didst devote thy whole life to them; I beseech thee to be also my and my children's protector and advocate with Jesus thy adopted Son. Obtain for me the grace to fulfil my duties to my children as thou and Mary have done to Jesus. St. Joseph, pray for me. Amen.

A Prayer to the Guardian Angels.

O holy guardian angels, ye heavenly

friends of my children, full of confidence I turn to you. Those whom the Lord has entrusted to me he has also entrusted to your love and care. Obtain for me by your intercession, that animated with the same sentiment which animates you towards my children, I may do all things to bring them up for God and heaven. O may I be such a father to them that I may be not unworthy of your love and friendship. Obtain this for me by your powerful intercession. Amen.

A Prayer to the Patron Saints of the Children.*

Holy patrons of my children, St. ——— and St. ———, take an interest in me

---

* They too should be justly venerated and invoked, since they have in holy baptism been appointed, to be not only models for imitation, but also intercessors of the children. Hence also the direction of holy Church to give to the children not profane names but the names of *Saints.*

their father; pray for me that through your intercession I may receive the grace that I may by word and example exercise a salutary influence over my children, and that they, by imitating your virtues, may grow up good members of the Church and be received one day into your happy society. Amen.

A Father's Prayer for Blessings on his Work.

O God, all that I may do for the proper education of my children will not bear fruit without the blessing of thy grace. Although I may "plant and water," the "increase" will be wanting if thou dost not "give" it. "Except the Lord build the house," says the Psalmist, "they labor in vain who build it. Except the Lord keep the city he watcheth in vain that keepeth it." Therefore I beseech thee, O Lord, give "the increase" to all that I do for my children by teaching, admonition, warning, punishment, vigilance and direction; assist me to "keep" them from all evil of body and soul; assist me to "build" that the "house" of virtue and perfection will have in them a firm foundation. Accompany my words and works with thy grace that they may conduce to the welfare of my children, through Jesus Christ. Amen.

A Prayer for Protection of the Children in Temptation.

O God, to how many and great temptations of body and soul are my children exposed! And how insufficient is the protection I can give them. Yes, Lord, "In vain I watch over them if thou dost not assist me." But if they dwell "in the aid of the Most High, and abide under the protection of the God of Jacob," how contented may I not be! Receive then, O Lord, my children, under thy protection. Keep them far from all dangers of soul and body; give them health. But above all protect them from danger to their souls. Keep far from them all that may exercise a hurtful influence on their young hearts and become an occasion of sin to them. Preserve them from sin. Send "thy holy angels to keep them in all their ways that they may bear them up in their hands, lest they dash their feet against a stone." O Almighty God and father, lead my children through the dangers and storms of this life, that they may enter safely into the haven of salvation. Amen.

A Prayer to Preserve the Children from Mortal Sin.

O God, how many and how great are the temptations to sin for my children in this world! And it is not in my power to lead them safely through them Thou must assist and protect, thou mus rescue and lead to victory. Come then to my aid, O Lord, in the power of thy grace, that the monster of mortal sin may not approach my children. Thou knowest, O Lord, how much I love my children; but I would rather that thou shouldst take them from me by death than that by sin they should suffer the death of their souls and become an object of abomination and wrath to thee. Therefore I beseech thee, thou Father of my children, haste to take them out of this life rather than that they should suffer this misfortune, so that by losing them during this short life I may find them again in thy house and possess them forever with thee. Hear me, O Lord, hear me; through Jesus Christ our Lord. Amen.—Hail Mary.

A Prayer for Purity in Children.

O most holy God, who lovest purity and innocence, grant my children the precious gift of purity. Alas, if the vice of impurity should soil my children. How unhappy would they be—for time and eternity. Lord, protect them; keep far from them this terrible misfortune!

Without thy special grace they cannot preserve holy purity. O Lord, grant them this grace! May their hearts be as a sanctuary undefiled by any impure thoughts and sentiments; may their eyes be modest, their ears and mouth closed to any impropriety in word or conversation; fill them with horror for everything contrary to purity, and let them, unblemished in body and soul, continue to be temples consecrated to the Holy Ghost. O Lord, thou lover of pure souls, let my children be numbered among thy beloved ones; let that blessing which in time and eternity accompanies holy purity come to my children.

Immaculate Mother, thou model and intercessor of pure souls; St. Joseph, St. Aloysius, and all holy youths, virgins, and saintly children, help me by your intercession. Amen.

Prayer of a Christian Father for his Wife.

O God, who, next to me, hast entrusted my children to my wife, hear my prayer for her. How great is the influence which she as mother has over the children; grant that she may be a faithful and true Christian mother to our children. Give her the spirit of piety and the fear of the Lord; fill her heart more and more with love for thee and for her children, that she may bring them up for thee, and by word and example lead them to a truly Christian life, and to eternal happiness. Assist her that she may not sink under the sacrifices and difficulties of her maternal vocation; visit her with the consolations of thy grace. Bless her labors in behalf of her children, that they may grow up pleasing in thy sight and be our joy and consolation. Thou art a liberal rewarder; reward then my wife with grace and eternal life for what she does for our children, who are also thine. Amen.

Litany of the Christian Father.

Lord have mercy on me!
Christ have mercy on me!
Lord have mercy on me!
Christ, hear me!

Thou great Father, from whom all fatherhood proceeds,
God, the heavenly Father of my children,
Thou who lovest my children more than I can,
Thou who willest them to be eternally happy with thee,
Thou who hast sacrificed thy only begotten Son for them,
Thou who sendest thy angels to protect them,
Thou who hast entrusted them to my love and care,
Thou who willest me to support and bring them up for thee,
Thou who will require an account of them from me,
Thou who will reward the father who fulfils his duty,
God the Son, Redeemer of the world,
Thou who becamest man for us,
O Jesus, who by becoming a child hast sanctified the tender age of childhood,

} Have mercy on me.

Prayers. 267

O Jesus, most loving child,
O Jesus, most obedient son of thy mother,
O Jesus, friend of children,
'O Jesus, who didst permit little children to come to thee, to embrace and bless them,
Thou who hast declared woe to all who scandalize children,
Thou who acceptest as done for thee what is done for children,
Thou who lovest my children and sacrificed thyself for them,
Thou who hast endowed thy church with all the treasures of grace for them,
Thou who, in the sacrament of marriage, didst bless me and give me grace to fulfil my vocation,
Thou who in holy baptism madest my children, children of God,
Thou without whose grace I cannot do my duty to my children,
Thou without whose grace my children cannot become good and persevere,
Thou spirit of wisdom and understanding,
Thou spirit of counsel and of strength,
Thou spirit of godliness and the fear of the Lord,
Thou spirit of wisdom and of grace,
Holy Trinity, one God,

Have mercy on me!

Holy Mary,
Holy Mother of God,
Mother of Christ,
Thou who didst offer thy divine Son in the Temple,
Thou who didst flee with him into Egypt,
Thou who soughtest him in sorrow for three days,
Thou who didst behold him suffering and dying on the cross,
Thou who didst rejoice in his resurrection and ascension,
Thou who art now glorified with him in heaven,
St. Joseph,
Thou patron of the Christian family,
Thou who didst protect and cherish thy divine foster-Son,
Thou who hadst the happiness of living and working so many years with him,
Thou who didst breathe thy last in his arms,
Ye holy guardian angels and friends of my children, who look upon the face of our heavenly Father,
Ye who are sent by God to guard my children,
St. Joachim, consort of St. Anna and father of the Blessed Virgin Mary,

} *Pray for me.*

All ye holy fathers of the old law,
All holy fathers,
Ye who by fulfilling your duties to your children obtained salvation,
All ye holy angels,
All ye patriarchs and prophets,
All ye holy apostles and martyrs,
All ye holy bishops, priests, and confessors,
All ye holy virgins and widows,
All ye holy and innocent children,
} *Pray for me.*

Be merciful and spare me, O Lord!
Be merciful and hear me, O Lord!

From all evil,
From all indifference to the duties of my vocation,
From all neglect of my paternal duties.
From all indifference to the salvation of my children,
From all unreasonable love and indulgence for my children,
From all anger and passion,
From all bad example,
From the demon of impurity,
By thy life, sufferings, and death,
By thy love for children,
By the rich reward thou didst promise them who receive children,
By the mercy of thy divine heart,
} *Deliver me, O Lord.*

I, a sinner, beseech thee to hear me.

That thou grant me grace to know the grandeur of my fatherly vocation,
That thou grant me to know the holiness and importance of my duties to my children,
That thou grant me wisdom to know my difficult task,
That thou grant me zeal in prayer for my children,
That thou bless my teachings and admonitions,
That thou grant me grace to always give my children good example,
That thou guard my children from all frivolity and mortal sin,
That thou inspire them with piety and the fear of God,
That thou grant them the treasure of inviolate purity,
That thou guard them from the attack of the enemy,
That thou guard them from the evil influence of the world,
That thou keep them in thy grace,
That thou lead them to eternal life,
} I beseech thee to hear me.

Lamb of God, who takest away the sins of the world, spare me!
Lamb of God, who takest, etc., hear me.

Lamb of God, who takest, etc., have mercy on me.
Christ, hear us, etc.
Our Father, Hail Mary.

PRAYER.—O God, whose mercy and goodness are infinite, I thank thy majesty for all the gifts and graces thou hast granted me and my children; and as thou grantest the prayers of those who beseech thee I pray unceasingly to thy fatherly kindness never to forsake me and my children, and lead us to eternal reward. Through Jesus Christ. Amen.

Prayer to the Sacred Heart of Jesus.

O most Sacred Heart of Jesus, Abode of the most perfect love, containing all perfection; worthy to be honored above all things by all hearts, I also offer unto Thee my sincere veneration; I love Thee with my whole heart, and I wish nothing else but to love Thee more and more, in order to consecrate to Thee all that I have and am.

O divine Heart, filled with so great and loving a care for men that Thou hast ordained and accomplished whatever was useful for their true welfare, and delivered Thyself up to ignominy and suffering, and even to death, for their sake, awake also in my heart similar sentiments of love, so that I too may be ready to offer sacrifices for the good of my neighbor, and to undergo troubles and difficulties. Inspire my heart especially with love for my children, similar to that which Thou hast for them, so that I may live wholly for them, and like Thee make every effort to lead them to eternal salvation.

To Thy loving Heart, O Jesus, I recommend my children. Encircle them, sanctuary of love, with Thy burning flames. Keep them so that no one may tear them from Thee. Thou knowest the dangers to which they are exposed, the enemies which threaten them. Have pity on them! According to the multitude of Thy mercies, hasten to their assistance. O most Sacred Heart of my Lord, wherein are contained all virtues and perfections, free my children from whatever is displeasing to Thee; destroy in them sin, and pardon them all the evil they have committed against Thee. Infuse into them out of Thy most Sacred Heart whatever is pleasing to Thee. Sanctify and take possession of them. Do in all things in their regard what is most pleasing to Thee, only preserve them in Thy holy love; cast them not away from Thee, I implore Thee. Grant that they may be united to Thee for all eternity in love and happiness. Amen.

Prayer to the Sacred Heart of Mary.

O sacred heart of Mary, Mother of God and our Mother, heart most pleasing to the adorable Trinity, and worthy the veneration and love of angels and men; O heart most like the sacred heart of Jesus whose perfect image thou art; heart full of kindness and compassion for our misery: to thee I commend myself in the holiest work of my life—the education of my children. To thee, O most loving heart of Mary, I commend my children; through thy intercession thou canst do all things. Infuse into them a love for thy virtues, and enkindle in them that holy fire by which thou wert always inflamed. Watch over them, guard them, and be to them always a refuge and an invincible barrier against the assaults of the enemy. Be their help in need, their strength in distress, their refuge in temptations, their protector in danger; be a mother to them; reconcile them with thy Son, commend them to thy Son, present them to thy Son. Assist them now and at all times, particularly at the hour of death, O kind, O mild, O sweet Virgin Mary. Amen.

Prayer to St. Aloysius.

O Saint Aloysius, thou who by the most perfect co-operation with grace hast led a truly angelic life, and who art venerated by the Church as the model and patron of youth, I commend to thee also my children; approach the throne of God in their behalf. Pray for them, that they also may walk in the commandments of the Lord and hate and shun sin as thou hast done. Obtain for them the grace of that innocence and purity of heart which adorned thy life; help them that they may honor and love the Lord and his Blessed mother as devoutly as thou hast. Saint Aloysius, pray for them. Amen.

STANDARD CATHOLIC BOOKS

PUBLISHED BY

BENZIGER BROTHERS,

CINCINNATI:	NEW YORK:	CHICAGO:
343 MAIN ST.	36 & 38 BARCLAY ST.	211-213 MADISON ST.

DOCTRINE, INSTRUCTION, DEVOTION.

ABANDONMENT; or, Absolute Surrender. Caussade. *net*, 0 40
ALPHONSUS LIGUORI, ST. Works. 22 vols., each, *net*, 1 25
ANALYSIS OF THE GOSPELS. Rev. L. A. Lambert, LL.D. *net*, 1 25
APOSTLES' CREED, THE. Rev. Müller, C.SS.R. *net*, 1 10
ART OF PROFITING BY OUR FAULTS. Rev. J. Tissot. *net*, 0 40
BIBLE, THE HOLY. 0 80
BIRTHDAY SOUVENIR. Mrs. A. E. Buchanan. 0 50
BLESSED VIRGIN, THE. Rev. Dr. Keller. 0 75
BLOSSOMS OF THE CROSS. Emmy Giehrl. 1 25
BOOK OF THE PROFESSED. Vol. I., *net*, 0 75; Vol. II., *net*, 0.60; Vol. III., *net*, 0 60
BOYS' AND GIRLS' MISSION BOOK. By the Redemptorist Fathers. 0 35
CATECHISM EXPLAINED, THE. Spirago-Clarke. *net*, 2 50
CATHOLIC BELIEF. Faa di Bruno. Paper, 0.25; 100 copies, $15.00. Cloth, 0.50; 25 copies, 7 50
CATHOLIC CEREMONIES. Abbé Durand. Paper, 0.30; 25 copies, $4.50. Cloth, 0.60; 25 copies, 9 00
CATHOLIC PRACTICE AT CHURCH AND AT HOME. Klauder. Paper, 0.30; 25 copies, $4.50. Cloth, 0.60; 25 copies, 9 00
CATHOLIC TEACHING FOR CHILDREN. Winifride Wray. 0 40
CATHOLIC WORSHIP. Rev. R. Brennan, LL.D. Paper, 0.15; 100 copies, $10.00. Cloth, 0.25; 100 copies, 17 00

I

CHARACTERISTICS OF TRUE DEVOTION. Grou, S.J.
  net, 0 75
CHARITY THE ORIGIN OF EVERY BLESSING. 0 60
CHILD OF MARY. Prayer-Book for Children. 0 60
CHILD'S PRAYER-BOOK OF THE SACRED HEART. 0 20
CHRISTIAN FATHER. Right Rev. W. Cramer.
  Paper, 0.25; 25 copies, $3.75. Cloth, 0.40;
  25 copies, 6 00
CHRISTIAN MOTHER. Right Rev. W. Cramer.
  Paper, 0.25; 25 copies, $3.75. Cloth, 0.40;
  25 copies, 6 00
CHURCH AND HER ENEMIES. Rev. M. Müller,
  C.SS.R. *net*, 1 10
COMEDY OF ENGLISH PROTESTANTISM. A. F. Marshall. *net*, 0 75
COMPLETE OFFICE OF HOLY WEEK, 0.50; 100 copies, 35 00
COMMUNION. Edited by Rev. John J. Nash, D.D.
  Per 100, *net*, 3 50
CONFESSION. Edited by Rev. John J. Nash, D.D.
  Per 100, *net*, 3 50
CONFIRMATION. Edited by Rev. John J. Nash, D.D.
  Per 100, *net*, 3 50
DEVOTION OF THE HOLY ROSARY and the Five Scapulars. *net*, 0 75
DEVOTIONS AND PRAYERS FOR THE SICK-ROOM. Krebs. *net*, 1 00
DEVOTIONS AND PRAYERS OF ST. ALPHONSUS. 1 00
DEVOTIONS for the First Friday. Huguet. 0 40
DEVOUT INSTRUCTIONS, GOFFINE'S. $1.00; 25 copies, 17 50
DIGNITY AND DUTY OF THE PRIEST. Liguori.
  net, 1 25
DIGNITY, AUTHORITY, DUTIES OF PARENTS, ECCLESIASTICAL AND CIVIL POWERS. Rev. M. Müller, C.SS.R. *net*, 1 40
DIVINE OFFICE, THE. Liguori. *net*, 1 25
EPISTLES AND GOSPELS. 0.25; 100 copies, 19 00
EUCHARIST AND PENANCE. Rev. M. Müller, C.SS.R.
  net, 1 10
EUCHARISTIC CHRIST, THE. Rev. A. Tesnière.
  net, 1 00
EUCHARISTIC GEMS. Coelenbier. 0 75
EXPLANATION OF COMMANDMENTS, ILLUSTRATED. 1 00
EXPLANATION OF THE APOSTLES' CREED, ILLUSTRATED. 1 00
EXPLANATION OF THE BALTIMORE CATECHISM. Kinkead. *net*, 1 00

EXPLANATION OF THE COMMANDMENTS. Müller, C.SS.R. *net*, 1 10
EXPLANATION OF THE GOSPELS. Lambert. Paper, 0.30; 25 copies, $4.50. Cloth, 0.60; 25 copies, 9 00
EXPLANATION OF THE HOLY SACRAMENTS, ILLUSTRATED. 1 00
EXPLANATION OF THE MASS. Cochem. 1 25
EXPLANATION OF THE OUR FATHER AND THE HAIL MARY. 0 75
EXPLANATION OF THE PRAYERS AND CEREMONIES OF THE MASS, ILLUSTRATED. Rev. D. I. Lanslots, O.S.B. 1 25
EXPLANATION OF THE SALVE REGINA. Liguori. 0 75
EXTREME UNCTION. 0.10; 100 copies, 6 00
FAMILIAR EXPLANATION OF CATHOLIC DOCTRINE. Müller. 1 00
FIRST AND GREATEST COMMANDMENT. Rev. M. Müller, C.SS.R. *net*, 1 40
FIRST COMMUNICANT'S MANUAL. 0.50; 100 copies, 25 00
FLOWERS OF THE PASSION. Thoughts of St. Paul of the Cross. 0.50; per 100 copies, 30 00
FOLLOWING OF CHRIST. Thomas à Kempis.
  With Reflections, 0.50; 100 copies, 25 00
  Without Reflections, 0.45; 100 copies, 22 50
  Edition de luxe, 1 50
FOUR LAST THINGS, THE. Cochem. Cloth, 0 75
GARLAND OF PRAYER. With Nuptial Mass. Leather, 0 90
GENERAL CONFESSION MADE EASY. Rev. A. Konings, C.SS.R. Flexible. 0.15; 100 copies, 10 00
GENERAL PRINCIPLES OF THE RELIGIOUS LIFE. Verheyen. *net*, 0 30
GLORIES OF DIVINE GRACE. Dr. M. J. Scheeben. *net*, 1 50
GLORIES OF MARY. St. Alphonsus de Liguori. 2 vols., *net*, 2 50
GOFFINE'S DEVOUT INSTRUCTIONS. 140 Illustrations. Cloth, $1.00; 25 copies, 17 50
GOLDEN SANDS. Little Counsels for the Sanctification and Happiness of Daily Life.
  Third Series, 0 50
  Fourth Series, 0 50
  Fifth Series, 0 50
GRACE AND THE SACRAMENTS. Müller. *net*, 1 25
GREAT MEANS OF SALVATION AND OF PERFECTION. Liguori. *net*, 1 25

GREAT SUPPER OF GOD, THE. A Treatise on Weekly Communion. Rev. S. Coubé, S.J. Edited by Rev. F. X. Brady, S.J. Cloth, *net*, 1 00
GREETINGS TO THE CHRIST-CHILD. Illustrated. 0 60
GUIDE TO CONFESSION AND COMMUNION. 0 60
HANDBOOK OF THE CHRISTIAN RELIGION. Wilmers. *net*, 1 50
HAPPY YEAR, A. Abbé Lasausse. *net*, 1 00
HEART OF ST. JANE FRANCES DE CHANTAL. *net*, 0 40
HELP FOR THE POOR SOULS IN PURGATORY. 0 50
HIDDEN TREASURE. St. Leonard Pt. Maurice. 0 50
HISTORY OF THE MASS. O'Brien. *net*, 1 25
HOLY EUCHARIST. Liguori. *net*, 1 25
HOLY MASS. Müller. *net*, 1 25
HOLY MASS. Liguori. *net*, 1 25
HOW TO COMFORT THE SICK. Krebs. *net*, 1 00
HOW TO MAKE THE MISSION. Paper, 0.10; per 100, 5 00
ILLUSTRATED PRAYER-BOOK FOR CHILDREN. 0.25; 100 copies, 17 00
IMITATION OF CHRIST. See "Following of Christ."
IMITATION OF THE BLESSED VIRGIN MARY. Translated by Mrs. A. R. Bennett-Gladstone. Plain Edition, 0.50. Edition de luxe, 1 50
IMITATION OF THE SACRED HEART. Rev. F. Arnoudt, S.J. 1 25
INCARNATION, BIRTH, AND INFANCY OF JESUS CHRIST. Liguori. *net*, 1 25
INDULGENCES, A PRACTICAL GUIDE TO. Rev. P. M. Bernad, O.M.I. 0 75
IN HEAVEN WE KNOW OUR OWN. Blot. 0 60
INSTRUCTIONS AND PRAYERS FOR THE CATHOLIC FATHER. Egger. 0 50
INSTRUCTIONS AND PRAYERS FOR THE CATHOLIC MOTHER. Egger. 0 50
INSTRUCTIONS on the Principal Truths of Our Holy Religion. Ward. *net*, 0 75
INSTRUCTIONS FOR FIRST COMMUNICANTS. Schmitt. *net*, 0 50
INSTRUCTIONS ON THE COMMANDMENTS OF GOD. Liguori. Paper, 0.25; 100 copies, $12.50. Cloth, 0.40; 100 copies, 21 00
INTERIOR OF JESUS AND MARY. Grou. 2 vols., *net*, 2 00
INTRODUCTION TO A DEVOUT LIFE. St. Francis de Sales. Cloth, 0.50; 100 copies, 30 00
JESUS THE GOOD SHEPHERD. De Goesbriand. *net*, 0 75

LABORS OF THE APOSTLES. De Goesbriand. *net*, 1 00
LETTERS OF ST. ALPHONSUS DE LIGUORI. 4 vols.,
each, *net*, 1 25
LETTERS OF ST. ALPHONSUS LIGUORI and General
Alphabetical Index to His Works. *net*, 1 25
LITTLE BOOK OF SUPERIORS. *net*, 0 60
LITTLE CHILD OF MARY. A Prayer-Book. 0.35;
100 copies, 21 00
LITTLE MANUAL OF ST. ANTHONY. Illustrated.
0.60; 100 copies, 36 00
LITTLE MONTH OF MAY. Flexible, 0.25; 100 copies,
19 00
LITTLE MONTH OF THE SOULS IN PURGATORY. 0.25;
100 copies, 19 00
LITTLE OFFICE OF THE IMMACULATE CONCEPTION,
0.05; per 100, 2 50
LITTLE PRAYER-BOOK OF THE SACRED HEART. 0 40
MANIFESTATION OF CONSCIENCE. Langogne.
net, 0 50
MANUAL OF THE BLESSED VIRGIN. 0 50
MANUAL OF THE HOLY EUCHARIST. Lasance. 0 75
MANUAL OF THE HOLY FAMILY. 0 60
MARIAE COROLLA. Poems by Father Edmund of the
Heart of Mary, C.P. 1 25
MASS DEVOTIONS AND READINGS ON THE MASS. 0 75
MAXIMS AND COUNSELS OF FRANCIS DE SALES.
net, 0 35
MAY DEVOTIONS, NEW. Wirth. *net*, 1 00
MEANS OF GRACE. Rev. Richard Brennan,
LL.D. 2 50
MEDITATIONS FOR EVERY DAY. Hamon, SS. 5 vols.,
net, 5 00
MEDITATIONS FOR EVERY DAY IN THE YEAR. Baxter.
net, 1 25
MEDITATIONS FOR EVERY DAY. Vercruysse, S.J.
2 vols., *net*, 2 75
MEDITATIONS FOR RETREATS. St. Francis de Sales.
Cloth, *net*, 0 75
MEDITATIONS ON THE FOUR LAST THINGS. Cochem.
0 75
MEDITATIONS ON THE LAST WORDS FROM THE CROSS.
Perraud. *net*, 0 50
MEDITATIONS ON THE LIFE, THE TEACHINGS, AND
THE PASSION OF JESUS CHRIST. Ilg-Clarke. 2
vols., *net*, 3 50
MEDITATIONS ON THE MONTH OF OUR LADY. 0 75
MEDITATIONS ON THE PASSION OF OUR LORD. 0.40;
100 copies, 24 00

MEDITATIONS ON THE SUFFERINGS OF JESUS CHRIST.
Rev. Francis da Perinaldo. net, 0 75
MISCELLANY. Historical Sketch of the Congregation of the Most Holy Redeemer. Rules and Constitutions of the Congregation of the Most Holy Redeemer. Instructions on the Religious State. St. Alphonsus de Liguori. net, 1 25
MISSION BOOK FOR THE MARRIED. Very Rev. F. Girardey, C.SS.R. 0.50; 100 copies, 25 00
MISSION BOOK FOR THE SINGLE. Very Rev. F. Girardey, C.SS.R. 0.50; 100 copies, 25 00
MISSION BOOK OF THE REDEMPTORIST FATHERS. 0.50; 100 copies, 25 00
MISTRESS OF NOVICES, THE. Leguay. net, 0 75
MOMENTS BEFORE THE TABERNACLE. Russell, S.J. net, 0 40
MONTH, NEW, OF ST. JOSEPH. St. Francis de Sales. 0 25
MONTH, NEW, OF THE HOLY ANGELS. St. Francis de Sales. 0 25
MONTH, NEW, OF THE SACRED HEART. St. Francis de Sales. 0 25
MONTH OF MAY; a Series of Meditations. Debussi, S.J. 0 50
MONTH OF THE DEAD. Cloquet. 0 50
MOST HOLY ROSARY. Thirty-one Meditations. Cramer. 0 50
MOST HOLY SACRAMENT. Rev. Dr. Jos. Keller. 0 75
MY FIRST COMMUNION: The Happiest Day of My Life. Brennan. 0 75
NEW RULE OF THE THIRD ORDER. 0.05; per 100, 3 00
NEW TESTAMENT. Cheap Edition. 32mo, flexible cloth, net, 0 15
NEW TESTAMENT. Illustrated Edition. 24mo, garnet cloth, with 100 full-page illustrations, net, 0 60
NEW TESTAMENT. India Paper Edition. 3003 Lambskin, limp, round corners, gilt edges, net, 1 00
NEW TESTAMENT. Large Print Edition. 12mo, cloth, round corners, red edges, net, 0 75
NEW TESTAMENT STUDIES. Right Rev. Mgr. Thomas J. Conaty, D.D. 12mo, 0 60
OFFICE, COMPLETE, OF HOLY WEEK. 0.50; 100 copies, 35 00
ON THE ROAD TO ROME. W. Richards. net, 0 50
OUR BIRTHDAY BOUQUET. E. C. Donnelly. 1 00

OUR FAVORITE DEVOTIONS. Lings. 0 60
OUR FAVORITE NOVENAS. Lings. 0 60
OUR LADY OF GOOD COUNSEL IN GENAZZANO. Dillon, D.D. 0 75
OUR MONTHLY DEVOTIONS. Very Rev. Dean A. A. Lings. 1 25
OUR OWN WILL. Rev. John Allen, D.D. *net,* 0 75
PARACLETE, THE. Devotions to the Holy Ghost. 0 60
PARADISE ON EARTH OPEN TO ALL. Natale, S.J. *net,* 0 40
PASSION AND DEATH OF JESUS CHRIST. Liguori. *net,* 1 25
PASSION FLOWERS. Poems by Father Edmund of the Heart of Mary, C.P. 1 25
PEARLS FROM THE CASKET OF THE SACRED HEART. 0 50
PEOPLE'S MISSION BOOK, THE. Paper, 0.10; per 100, 6 00
PERFECT RELIGIOUS. De la Motte. Cloth, *net,* 1 00
PICTORIAL LIVES OF THE SAINTS. 1.00; 25 copies, 17 50
PIOUS PREPARATION FOR FIRST HOLY COMMUNION. Lasance. 0 75
POPULAR INSTRUCTIONS ON MARRIAGE. Girardey, C.SS.R. Paper, 0.25; 25 copies, $3.75. Cloth, 0.40; 25 copies, 6 00
POPULAR INSTRUCTIONS ON PRAYER. Girardey, C.SS.R. Paper, 0.25; 25 copies, $3.75. Cloth, 0.40; 25 copies, 6 00
POPULAR INSTRUCTIONS TO PARENTS. Girardey, C.SS.R. Paper, 0.25; 25 copies, $3.75. Cloth, 0.40; 25 copies, 6 00
PRAYER-BOOK FOR LENT. Gethsemani, Jerusalem, and Golgotha. Rev. A. Geyer. 0 50
PRAYER. The Great Means of Obtaining Salvation. By St. Alphonsus de Liguori. 0 50
PREACHING. Liguori. *net,* 1 25
PREPARATION FOR DEATH. Liguori. *net,* 1 25
PRODIGAL SON; or, The Sinner's Return to God. *net,* 1 00
RELIGIOUS STATE, THE. St. Alphonsus de Liguori. 0 50
REVELATIONS OF THE SACRED HEART to Blessed Margaret Mary. Bougaud. Cloth, *net,* 1 50
SACRAMENTALS OF THE HOLY CATHOLIC CHURCH. Rev. A. A. Lambing, D.D. Paper, 0.30; 25 copies, $4.50. Cloth, 0.60; 25 copies, 9 00

SACRAMENTALS—Prayer, etc. Müller. *net*, 1 00
SACRED HEART, THE. Rev. Dr. Joseph Keller. 0 75
SACRED HEART, THE. Studies in the Sacred Scriptures. Saintrain, C.SS.R. *net*, 2 00
SACRIFICE OF THE MASS WORTHILY CELEBRATED, THE. Chaignon, S.J. *net*, 1 50
SECRET OF SANCTITY. St. Francis de Sales.
net, 1 00
SERAPHIC GUIDE, THE. 0 60
SHORT CONFERENCES ON THE LITTLE OFFICE OF THE IMMACULATE CONCEPTION. Rainer. 0 50
SHORT STORIES ON CHRISTIAN DOCTRINE. *net*, 0 75
SODALISTS' VADE MECUM. 0 50
SONGS AND SONNETS. Maurice Francis Egan. 1 00
SOUVENIR OF THE NOVITIATE. Taylor. *net*, 0 60
SPIRITUAL CRUMBS FOR HUNGRY LITTLE SOULS. Mary E. Richardson. 0 50
SPIRITUAL DIRECTION. *net*, 0 60
SPIRITUAL EXERCISES FOR TEN DAYS' RETREAT. Smetana, C.SS.R. *net*, 1 00
ST. ANTHONY. Rev. Dr. Jos. Keller. 0 75
ST. JOSEPH, OUR ADVOCATE. By Father Huguet.
0 90
STATIONS OF THE CROSS. Illustrated. 0 50
STORIES FOR FIRST COMMUNICANTS. Keller, D.D.
0 50
STRIVING AFTER PERFECTION. Bayma, S.J. *net*, 1 00
SURE WAY TO A HAPPY MARRIAGE. Taylor. Paper, 0.25; 25 copies, $3.75. Cloth, 0.40; 25 copies, 6 00
THOUGHT FROM BENEDICTINE SAINTS. *net*, 0 35
THOUGHT FROM ST. ALPHONSUS. *net*, 0 35
THOUGHT FROM ST. FRANCIS OF ASSISI and His Saints. *net*, 0 35
THOUGHT FROM ST. IGNATIUS. *net*, 0 35
THOUGHT FROM ST. TERESA. *net*, 0 35
THOUGHT FROM ST. VINCENT DE PAUL. *net*, 0 35
THOUGHTS AND COUNSELS for the Consideration of Catholic Young Men. Rev. P. A. Doss, S.J.
net, 1 25
TRUE POLITENESS. Abbé Francis Demore. *net*, 0 60
TRUE SPOUSE OF JESUS CHRIST. Liguori. 2 vols., Centenary Edition, *net*, $2.50. The same in one volume, *net*, 1 00
TWO SPIRITUAL RETREATS FOR SISTERS. Zollner.
net, 1 00
VENERATION OF THE BLESSED VIRGIN. Rohner, O.S.B. 1 25
VICTORIES OF THE MARTYRS. Liguori. *net*, 1 25

VISITS TO JESUS IN THE TABERNACLE. Lasance.
Cloth, 1 25
VISITS TO THE MOST HOLY SACRAMENT. Liguori.
0 50
VOCATIONS EXPLAINED. 0.10; 100 copies, 6 00
WAY OF INTERIOR PEACE. De Lehen, S.J. net, 1 25
WAY OF SALVATION AND PERFECTION. Liguori.
net, 1 25
WAY OF THE CROSS. Paper, 0.05; 100 copies, 2 50
WORDS OF WISDOM. A Concordance to the Sapiential Books. Edited by Rev. John J. Bell.
net, 1 25
YEAR OF THE SACRED HEART. A Thought for Every Day of the Year. Anna T. Sadlier. 0 50
YOUNG GIRLS' BOOK OF PIETY AT SCHOOL AND AT HOME. 1 00

JUVENILES.

ADVENTURES OF A CASKET. 0 45
ADVENTURES OF A FRENCH CAPTAIN. 0 45
AN ADVENTURE WITH THE APACHES. Gabriel Ferry. 0 40
ANTHONY. A Tale of the Time of Charles II. of England. 0 45
ARMORER OF SOLINGEN. William Herchenbach. 0 40
BERTHA; or, Consequences of a Fault. 0 45
BEST FOOT FORWARD. Father Finn. 0 85
BETTER PART. 0 45
BISTOURI. A. Melandri. 0 40
BLACK LADY, AND ROBIN RED BREAST. Canon Schmid. 0 25
BLANCHE DE MARSILLY. 0 45
BLISSYLVANIA POST-OFFICE. Marion Ames Taggart. 0 40
BOYS IN THE BLOCK. Maurice F. Egan. 0 25
BRIC-A-BRAC DEALER. 0 45
BUZZER'S CHRISTMAS. Mary T. Waggaman. 0 25
BY BRANSCOME RIVER. Marion Ames Taggart.
0 40
CAKE AND THE EASTER EGGS. Canon Schmid. 0 25
CANARY BIRD. Canon Schmid. 0 40
CAPTAIN ROUGEMONT. 0 45
CASSILDA; or, The Moorish Princess. 0 45
CAVE BY THE BEECH FORK, THE. Rev. H. S. Spalding, S.J. 0 85
COLLEGE BOY, A. Anthony Yorke. Cloth, 0 85
CONVERSATIONS ON HOME EDUCATION. 0 45

Dimpling's Success. Clara Mulholland. 0 40
Episodes of the Paris Commune. An Account
   of the Religious Persecution. 0 45
Every-Day Girl, An. Mary C. Crowley. 0 40
Fatal Diamonds. E. C. Donnelly. 0 25
Finn, Rev. F. J., S.J.:
   His First and Last Appearance. Illustrated.
      1 00
   The Best Foot Forward. 0 85
   That Football Game. 0 85
   Ethelred Preston. 0 85
   Claude Lightfoot. 0 85
   Harry Dee. 0 85
   Tom Playfair. 0 85
   Percy Wynn. 0 85
   Mostly Boys. 0 85
Fisherman's Daughter. 0 45
Five O'Clock Stories. 0 75
Flower of the Flock, The. Maurice F. Egan.
   0 85
Fred's Little Daughter. Sara T. Smith. 0 40
Gertrude's Experience. 0 45
Godfrey the Hermit. Schmid. 0 25
Great Grandmother's Secret. 0 45
Heir of Dreams, An. S. M. O'Malley. 0 40
Her Father's Right Hand. 0 45
Hop Blossoms. Canon Schmid. 0 25
Hostage of War, A. Mary G. Bonesteel. 0 40
How They Worked Their Way. Maurice F.
   Egan. 0 75
Inundation, The. Canon Schmid. 0 40
Jack Hildreth on the Nile. Taggart. 0 85
Jack-o'-Lantern. Mary T. Waggaman. 0 40
Klondike Picnic. Eleanor C. Donnelly. 0 85
Lamp of the Sanctuary. Wiseman. 0 25
Legends of the Holy Child Jesus. 0 75
Little Missy. Mary T. Waggaman. 0 40
Loyal Blue and Royal Scarlet. Taggart. 0 85
Madcap Set at St. Anne's. Brunowe. 0 40
Marcelle. A True Story. 0 45
Master Fridolin. Emmy Giehrl. 0 25
Milly Aveling. Sara T. Smith. 0 85
Mysterious Doorway. Anna T. Sadlier. 0 40
My Strange Friend. Father Finn. 0 25
Nan Nobody. Mary T. Waggaman. 0 40
Old Charlmont's Seed-Bed. Sara T. Smith. 0 40
Old Robber's Castle. Canon Schmid. 0 25
Olive and the Little Cakes. 0 45

OVERSEER OF MAHLBOURG. Canon Schmid.	0 25
PANCHO AND PANCHITA. Mary E. Mannix.	0 40
PAULINE ARCHER. Anna T. Sadlier.	0 40
PICKLE AND PEPPER. Ella Loraine Dorsey.	0 85
PRIEST OF AUVRIGNY.	0 45
QUEEN'S PAGE. Katharine T. Hinkson.	0 40
RICHARD; or, Devotion to the Stuarts.	0 45
ROSE BUSH. Canon Schmid.	0 25
SEA-GULLS' ROCK. J. Sandeau.	0 40
SUMMER AT WOODVILLE. Anna T. Sadlier.	0 40
TALES AND LEGENDS OF THE MIDDLE AGES. F. de Capella.	0 75
TAMING OF POLLY. Ella Loraine Dorsey.	0 85
THREE GIRLS AND ESPECIALLY ONE. Marion A. Taggart.	0 40
THREE LITTLE KINGS. Emmy Giehrl.	0 25
TOM'S LUCK-POT. Mary T. Waggaman.	0 40
TREASURE OF NUGGET MOUNTAIN. Taggart.	0 85
VILLAGE STEEPLE, THE.	0 45
WINNETOU, THE APACHE KNIGHT. Taggart.	0 85
WRONGFULLY ACCUSED. William Herchenbach.	0 40

NOVELS AND STORIES.

ASER, THE SHEPHERD. A Christmas Story. Taggart.	net, 0 35
BEZALEEL. A Christmas Story. Taggart.	net, 0 35
CIRCUS RIDER'S DAUGHTER, THE. F. v. Brackel.	1 25
CONNOR D'ARCY'S STRUGGLES. Bertholds.	1 25
DION AND THE SIBYLS. Miles Keon.	1 25
FABIOLA. Wiseman. Popular Illustrated Edition, 0.90; Edition de luxe,	5 00
FABIOLA'S SISTERS. A. C. Clarke.	1 25
HEIRESS OF CRONENSTEIN, THE. Countess Hahn-Hahn.	1 25
IDOLS; or, The Secrets of the Rue Chaussée d'Antin. De Navery.	1 25
LET NO MAN PUT ASUNDER. A Novel. Josephine Marié.	1 00
LINKED LIVES. A Novel. Lady Gertrude Douglas.	1 50
MARCELLA GRACE. Rosa Mulholland. Illustrated Edition.	1 25
MISS ERIN. M. E. Francis.	1 25
MONK'S PARDON, THE. Raoul de Navery.	1 25
MR. BILLY BUTTONS. A Novel. Walter Lecky.	1 25
OUTLAW OF CAMARGUE, THE. Lamothe.	1 25
PASSING SHADOWS. Anthony Yorke.	1 25

Pere Monnier's Ward. Walter Lecky. 1 25
Petronilla. E. C. Donnelly. 1 00
Prodigal's Daughter, The. Lelia Hardin Bugg.
 1 00
Romance of a Playwright. De Bornier. 1 00
Round Table of the Representative American Catholic Novelists. Complete Stories, with Biographies, Portraits, etc. 1 50
Round Table of the Representative French Catholic Novelists. Complete Stories, with Biographies, Portraits, etc. 1 50
Round Table of the Representative Irish and English Catholic Novelists. Complete Stories, Biographies, Portraits, etc. 1 50
True Story of Master Gerard, The. Anna T. Sadlier. 1 25
Vocation of Edward Conway. Maurice F. Egan. 1 25
Woman of Fortune, A. Christian Reid. 1 25
World Well Lost. Esther Robertson. 0 75

LIVES AND HISTORIES.

Autobiography of St. Ignatius Loyola. Edited by Rev. J. F. X. O'Conor. Cloth, *net*, 1 25
Blessed Ones of 1888. With Illustrations, 0 50
Historiographia Ecclesiastica quam Historiæ seriam Solidamque Operam Navantibus, Accommodavit Guil. Stang, D.D. *net*, 1 00
History of the Catholic Church. Brueck. 2 vols. *net*, 3 00
History of the Catholic Church. Shea. 1 50
History of the Protestant Reformation. Cobbett. Cloth, *net*, 0.50; paper, *net*, 0 25
Letters of St. Alphonsus Liguori. Centenary Edition. 5 vols., each, *net*, 1 25
Life of Blessed Margaret Mary. Mgr. Bougaud. *net*, 1 50
Life of Christ. Illustrated. Cochem. 1 25
Life of Father Charles Sire. *net*, 1 00
Life of Father Jogues. *net*, 0 75
Life of Fr. Francis Poilvache. *net*, 0 20
Life of Mother Fontbonne. Abbé Rivaux. Cloth, *net*, 1 25
Life of Sister Anne Katherine Emmerich. Rev. Thomas Wegener, O.S.A. *net*, 1 50
Life of St. Aloysius Gonzaga, of the Society of Jesus. Rev. J. F. X. O'Conor, S.J. *net*, 0 75

LIFE OF ST. CATHARINE OF SIENA. Aymé. 1 00
LIFE OF ST. CLARE OF MONTEFALCO. Locke.
   net, 0 75
LIFE OF THE BLESSED VIRGIN. Illustrated. 1 25
LIFE OF THE VEN. MARY CRESCENTIA HOESS. Deymann, O.S.F. *net,* 1 25
LITTLE LIVES OF SAINTS FOR CHILDREN. Ill. 0 75
LOURDES. Clarke, S.J. 0 75
NAMES THAT LIVE IN CATHOLIC HEARTS. 1 00
OUR BIRTHDAY BOUQUET. Donnelly. 1 00
OUR LADY OF GOOD COUNSEL IN GENAZZANO. 0 75
OUTLINES OF JEWISH HISTORY, from Abraham to Our Lord. Rev. F. E. Gigot, S.S. *net,* 1 50
OUTLINES OF NEW TESTAMENT HISTORY. Rev. F. E. Gigot, S.S. Cloth, *net,* 1 50
PICTORIAL LIVES OF THE SAINTS. Cloth, 1 00
REMINISCENCES OF RT. REV. EDGAR P. WADHAMS, D.D. *net,* 1 00
ST. ANTHONY, THE SAINT OF THE WHOLE WORLD. Ward. 0 75
STORY OF THE DIVINE CHILD. A. A. Lings. 0 75
VICTORIES OF THE MARTYRS. Liguori. *net,* 1 25
VISIT TO EUROPE AND THE HOLY LAND. Fairbanks.
   1 50
WOMEN OF CATHOLICITY. Anna T. Sadlier. 1 00

THEOLOGY, LITURGY, SERMONS, SCIENCE, AND PHILOSOPHY.

ABRIDGED SERMONS. Liguori. *net,* 1 25
BAD CHRISTIAN, THE. Rev. F. Hunolt, S.J. Translated by Rev. J. Allen, D.D. 2 vols.,
   net, 5 00
BLESSED SACRAMENT, SERMONS ON THE. Rev. J. B. Scheurer, D.D. Edited by Rev. F. X. Lasance.
   net, 1 50
BREVE COMPENDIUM THEOLOGIAE DOGMATICAE ET MORALIS. Berthier, M.S. *net,* 2 50
BUSINESS GUIDE FOR PRIESTS. Stang. *net,* 0 85
CANONICAL PROCEDURE IN DISCIPLINARY AND CRIMINAL CASES OF CLERICS. Rev. F. Droste.
   net, 1 50
CHILDREN OF MARY, SERMONS FOR THE. Edited by R. F. Clarke, S.J. *net,* 1 50
CHRISTIAN ANTHROPOLOGY. Rev. John Thein.
   net, 2 50

CHRISTIAN PHILOSOPHY. A Treatise on the Human
Soul. Rev. J. T. Driscoll, S.T.L. *net*, 1 25
CHRISTIAN PHILOSOPHY: GOD. Driscoll. *net*, 1 25
CHRISTIAN'S LAST END, THE. Sermons. Rev.
F. Hunolt, S.J. Translated by Rev. J. Allen,
D.D. 2 vols., *net*, 5 00
CHRISTIAN'S MODEL, THE. Sermons. Rev. F.
Hunolt, S.J. Translated by Rev. J. Allen, D.D.
2 vols., *net*, 5 00
CHRISTIAN STATE OF LIFE, THE. Sermons.
Rev. F. Hunolt, S.J. Translated by Rev. J.
Allen, D.D. *net*, 5 00
CHRIST IN TYPE AND PROPHECY. Rev. A. J. Maas,
S.J. 2 vols. *net*, 4 00
CHURCH ANNOUNCEMENT BOOK. *net*, 0 25
CHURCH TREASURER'S PEW COLLECTION AND RE-
CEIPT BOOK. *net*, 1 00
COMMENTARIUM IN FACULTATES APOSTOLICAS EPIS-
COPIS necnon Vicariis et Praefectis Apostolicis
per Modum Formularum concedi solitas ad
usum Venerabilis Cleri, imprimis Americani con-
cinnatum ab Antonio Konings, C.SS.R. Edito
quarto, recognita in pluribus emendata et aucta,
curante Joseph Putzer, C.SS.R. *net*, 2 25
COMPENDIUM JURIS CANONICI, ad usum Cleri et
Seminariorum hujus Regionis accommodatum.
Auctori Rev. S. B. Smith, D.D. *net*, 2 00
COMPENDIUM SACRAE LITURGIAE JUXTA RITUM
ROMANUM. Wapelhorst, O.S.F. *net*, 2 50
CONFESSIONAL, THE. Roeggl. *net*, 1 00
DATA OF MODERN ETHICS EXAMINED. Ming, S.J.
net, 2 00
DE PHILOSOPHIA MORALI PRAELECTIONES quas in
Collegio Georgiopolitano Soc. Jesu, Anno 1889-90
Habuit P. Nicolaus Russo. *net*, 2 00
ECCLESIASTICAL DICTIONARY. Thein. *net*, 5 00
ELEMENTS OF ECCLESIASTICAL LAW. Smith.
ECCLESIASTICAL PERSONS. *net*, 2 50
ECCLESIASTICAL PUNISHMENTS. *net*, 2 50
ECCLESIASTICAL TRIALS. *net*, 2 50
FUNERAL SERMONS. Wirth. 2 vols. *net*, 2 00
GENERAL INTRODUCTION TO THE STUDY OF HOLY
SCRIPTURES. Gigot. Cloth, *net*, 2 00
GOD KNOWABLE AND KNOWN. Ronayne. *net*, 1 25
GOOD CHRISTIAN, THE. Sermons. Hunolt. Trans-
lated by Rev. J. Allen, D.D. 2 vols. *net*, 5 00
HISTORY OF THE MASS AND ITS CEREMONIES.
O'Brien. *net*, 1 25

LAST THINGS, SERMONS ON THE FOUR. Hunolt. Translated by Rev. John Allen, D.D. 2 vols.,
net, 5 00
LENTEN SERMONS. Wirth. *net*, 2 00
LIBER STATUS ANIMARUM; or, Parish Census Book. *Pocket Edition*, *net*, 0.25; half leather, *net*, 2 00
LITERARY, SCIENTIFIC, AND POLITICAL VIEWS OF ORESTES A. BROWNSON. Brownson. *net*, 1 25
MARRIAGE PROCESS IN THE UNITED STATES. Smith.
net, 2 50
MORAL PRINCIPLES AND MEDICAL PRACTICE, THE BASIS OF MEDICAL JURISPRUDENCE. By Rev. Charles Coppens, S.J. *net*, 1 50
NATURAL LAW AND LEGAL PRACTICE. Holaind, S.J.
net, 1 75
NEW AND OLD SERMONS. Wirth, O.S.B. 8 vols.,
net, 16 00
OFFICE OF TENEBRAE, THE. *net*, 0 50
OUR LORD, THE BLESSED VIRGIN, AND THE SAINTS, SERMONS ON. Rev. Francis Hunolt, S.J. Translated by Rev. John Allen, D.D. 2 vols.,
net, 5 00
OUTLINES OF DOGMATIC THEOLOGY. Rev. Sylvester Jos. Hunter, S.J. 3 vols., *net*, 4 50
OUTLINES OF NEW TESTAMENT HISTORY. Gigot. Cloth, *net*, 1 50
PASTORAL THEOLOGY. Rev. Wm. Stang, D.D.
net, 1 50
PENANCE, SERMONS ON. Rev. Francis Hunolt, S.J. Translated by Rev. John Allen. 2 vols.
net, 5 00
PENITENT CHRISTIAN, THE. Sermons. Rev. F. Hunolt. Translated by Rev. John Allen, D.D. 2 vols., *net*, 5 00
PEW-RENT RECEIPT BOOK. *net*, 1 00
PRAXIS SYNODALIS. Manuale Synodi Diocesanae ac Provincialis Celebrandae. *net*, 0 60
PRIEST IN THE PULPIT, THE. A Manual of Homiletics and Catechetics. Rev. B. Luebbermann. *net*, 1 50
REGISTRUM BAPTISMORUM. *net*, 3 50
REGISTRUM MATRIMONIORUM. *net*, 3 50
RITUALE COMPENDIOSUM seu Ordo Administrandi quaedam Sacramenta et alia Officia Ecclesiastica Rite Peragendi ex Rituali Romano, novissime edito desumptas. *net*, 0 75
ROSARY, SERMONS ON THE MOST HOLY. Frings.
net, 1 00

SACRED HEART, SIX SERMONS ON DEVOTION TO
THE. Rev. Dr. E. Bierbaum. *net*, 0 60
SANCTUARY BOYS' ILLUSTRATED MANUAL. Rev. J.
A. McCallen, S. S. *net*, 0 50
SERMON MANUSCRIPT BOOK. *net*, 2 00
SERMONS FOR THE SUNDAYS AND CHIEF FESTIVALS
OF THE ECCLESIASTICAL YEAR. Rev. J. Pott-
geisser, S.J. 2 vols., *net*, 2 50
SERMONS ON THE CHRISTIAN VIRTUES. Rev.
F. Hunolt, S.J. Translated by Rev. John Allen.
2 vols., *net*, 5 00
SERMONS ON THE DIFFERENT STATES OF LIFE.
Rev. F. Hunolt, S.J. Translated by Rev. John
Allen. 2 vols., *net*, 5 00
SERMONS ON THE SEVEN DEADLY SINS. Rev.
F. Hunolt, S.J. 2 vols. Translated by Rev.
John Allen, D.D. *net*, 5 00
SHORT SERMONS. Rev. F. Hunolt, S.J. 5 vols.,
10 00
SHORT SERMONS FOR LOW MASSES. Schouppe, S.J.
net, 1 25
SYNOPSIS THEOLOGIAE DOGMATICAE AD MENTEM S.
THOMAE AQUINATIS hodiernis moribus accom-
modata, auctore Ad. Tanquerey, S.S.:
1. THEOLOGIA FUNDAMENTALIS. Half morocco,
net, 1 50
2. THEOLOGIA DOGMATICA SPECIALIS. 2 vols.,
half morocco, *net*, 3 00
THEOLOGIA MORALIS NOVISSIMI ECCLESIAE DOC-
TORIS ALPHONSI. In Compendium Redacta, et
Usui Venerabilis Cleri Americani accommodata.
Auctore Rev. A. Konings, C.SS.R. Editio
septima, auctior et novis curis expolitior curante
Henrico Kuper, C.SS.R. 2 vols., *net*, 4 00
TWO-EDGED SWORD. Rev. Augustine Wirth,
O.S.B. Paper, *net*, 0 25
VADE MECUM SACERDOTUM, continens Preces ante
et post Missam, modum providendi infirmos,
necnon multas Benedictionum Formulas. Cloth,
net, 0.25; morocco flexible, *net*, 0 50
WHAT CATHOLICS HAVE DONE FOR SCIENCE. With
sketches of the Great Catholic Scientists.
Rev. Martin S. Brennan. 1 00

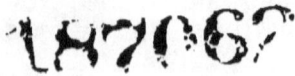

c/oi/c

www.ingramcontent.com/pod-product-compliance
Lightning Source LLC
Chambersburg PA
CBHW031332230426
43670CB00006B/323